CW00468512

WAVE CRE

EURIPIDES OF ATHENS

MEDEA

&

ALCESTIS

**Translated into English verse by
Michael James Gould**

GREEK DRAMA FOR TODAY

Wave Crest Classics
Ancient Greek Drama in Modern English Verse
Volume One
The Medea and Alcestis of Euripides
Translated by
Michael James Gould

For ELJ
χαιρουσα μοι

ISBN 0-9546457-0-7
Copyright © Michael James Gould 2003
Published by
Michael James Gould
Wave Crest Classics
12 Wave Crest Whitstable Kent CT5 1EH
michael@gould3.freeserve.co.uk

All enquiries re purchase of copies, royalties and
performance rights to be sent as above.

Printed by
Mickle Print Ltd
Westminster Road
Vauxhall Industrial Estate
Canterbury
Kent CT1 1YY

Wave Crest Classics

Volume One

The Medea and Alcestis of Euripides

CONTENTS

INTRODUCTION TO THE MEDEA OF EURIPIDES

This wonderful play saw its debut in the year 431 BC in ancient
Athens. I was privileged to study it for O-Level in 1964 AD under
the auspices of my Greek and Latin teacher, Mrs E L Jackson, to
whom this translation is dedicated. In rendering the play into
verse my intention is to bring the full flavour of it to as many
readers as possible. I say readers, but do not recommend silent
reading: if not declaimed on stage it should be read out loud.
*Please note that Medea should be pronounced to rhyme with "a
player".*

The story is as follows: Jason's wicked Uncle Pelias has murdered
Jason's father and claimed the throne of Iolcus, Thessaly, for
himself. (Near Volos on a modern map of Greece.) Jason has only
just escaped death by being smuggled out and brought up by
Cheiron, the Centaur. (Centaurs were mythical beings half man,
half horse.) Jason grows to adulthood and turns up to demand the
throne back, but gets sent off on a seemingly impossible quest for
the Golden Fleece. This item, to which the Greeks have some
claim, is kept under the guard of a sleepless serpent by King
Aeetes of Colchis, far away at the end of the known world, the
other side of the Black Sea, or Pontus as it was known in ancient
times. The ship he sails on is called the Argo and his crew, the
Argonauts.

Jason only succeeds in his task because Medea, the daughter of
King Aeetes, falls in love with him. She's a very clever lady, not
just skilled in all the natural sciences, but an enchantress and
magician, capable of putting spells on people and performing very
clever conjuring tricks, and she's quite without moral scruples. To
help Jason she has no qualms about betraying her father; and to
assist the Argo's escape, by gaining them more time, she kills her
brother Apsyrtus, who's been taken on board as hostage, and
throws his body in the sea. This obliges the Colchians to stop to
bury him.

Back in Iolcus she impresses the daughters of King Pelias with a
very clever piece of sorcery. She boils up a dead sheep and turns
it into a live young lamb. "I can do this for your dad," she
promises them, and they believe her. After killing their aged
father they are somewhat disappointed when Medea, as you might

expect, fails to restore his life and youth! Jason and Medea rule Iolcus for a while, but clearly Medea's style isn't too popular with the inhabitants, and they are deposed in a revolution. They then seek asylum in the city of Corinth, which is ruled by King Creon, and seem to live there together as a model couple in perfect harmony, until Creon offers Jason the hand of his daughter in marriage. This requires Jason to divorce Medea, which he is able to do quite easily, because Medea as a foreigner has no rights under Greek law.

At this point the curtain goes up. Medea is distraught, and in between her cries and moans vows vengeance on the king, his daughter and on Jason. Worse than that, in the opinion of her elderly female servant, the nurse, she is so severely unhinged she might even kill her own children. Medea discusses her problems with the women of Corinth, who form a chorus, commenting and singing throughout the play on the issues involved.

Medea's difficulties are then compounded by King Creon informing her that she must go into exile immediately with her two twin boys, as he is afraid of her reported threats. Medea, however, manages to persuade him to let her stay one day to make arrangements for her exile.

Then Jason comes on stage and very pompously denounces her for not seeing the good sense in his alliance with the King of Corinth. He brushes aside any suggestion as to what he owes her for the help she has given him, which he puts down to Cypris, the Goddess of Love, who just wanted to do him a favour by making Medea fall in love with him! He offers Medea some financial help, but does not seem terribly concerned about the loss of his children or their plight. She scornfully refuses his help, but what can she do?

Enter King Aegeus of Athens. He has been on a visit to the oracle at Delphi in connection with his lack of children. Medea confides her problems to him, and he swears to allow her to come and stay as his guest in Athens, subject to making her own way there, as he does not wish to offend his hosts in Corinth. Now that she has somewhere to go as a safe house this enables Medea to make her plans. She is going to get her children to take wedding gifts of a silken gown and golden head dress to Creon's daughter, and to beg to be allowed to stay in Corinth, whilst only Medea should go into exile. But this is just a ploy. The wedding gifts are to be poisoned, so that the daughter and all who touch her die; and then she intends to kill her children, both as an act of spite to Jason, and in case Creon's family should avenge Medea's crimes by killing the children themselves. No need to say any more! Read the play to see how Medea psyches herself up to do the deed, the Chorus deplore the wickedness and madness involved, the terrible events unfold and Jason is utterly destroyed.

Topics for study and discussion

What do you learn from this play about religion in ancient Greece?

What is the greatest gift the gods can offer?

What are the worst troubles that ever happen?

What feminist or women's issues do you find in the play?

How did the Greeks view non-Greeks?

How far do you feel sorry for Medea?

Do you think promises made under oath are more important than the laws we live by?

Did Medea think so? What are her motives? Can she help her actions?

What can you say about Jason? What opinions do you form of his character?

Does Medea manage to cast spells on, influence or manipulate any of the characters in the play?

Do you see any evidence of continuing affection by Jason towards Medea, despite his new marriage?

Do you see any differences in attitude of Jason towards his children in different parts of the play?

Why were our forefathers stupid and foolish?

Euripides was accused in his time of making his characters speak as people might in a formal debate, such as in a courtroom, or parliament. What evidence do you find of this in the play?

Do any of the characters behave like politicians?

Notes on Euripides.

Born in 485 BC and died in 406 BC he wrote 90 plays, of which 18 survive, as against a total of 14 other surviving tragedies of the contemporary playwrights Aeschylus and Sophocles. (A 19th play the Rhesus was attributed to Euripides, but modern scholars do not believe he wrote it.)
The plays were entered into dramatic festivals when prizes were awarded. In 22 contests he won 4 firsts. His contemporaries saw tragedy as occurring when a man was caught between the conflicting wills of different gods: Euripides, perhaps with less belief in those gods, saw human tragedy rather as arising from a conflict between passion and reason.

As Medea says:

"What I'm doing, though I know it,
That it's wicked, I can't help it;
For my passion's so much greater
Than my self control and reason;
That's what causes for us mortals
Far the most amount of evil."

THE MEDEA OF EURIPIDES

Characters of the Drama in order of appearance

Nurse

Medea's twin sons

Tutor

Medea

Chorus of the Women of Corinth

Creon, King of Corinth

Jason

Aegeus, King of Athens

Messenger

The play is set in front of Medea's house in Corinth.
Entrances from stage left are for persons coming from the King's
palace and the immediate neighbourhood;
From stage right are for travellers coming into Corinth.

Morning. The children's elderly nurse enters from Medea's house.

NURSE   Through the dark grey razor sharp rocks
How I wish the ship of Argo
Never flew to far off Colchis,
And the cut pines hadn't fallen
On the wooded slopes of Pelion,
Out of which the oars were fashioned
For the hands of men the finest,
Who went off to fetch the gold fleece
At the order of King Pelias.

Had this voyage never happened,
Poor Medea, who's my mistress,
Had not sailed to Iolcus Castle,
Heart on fire with love for Jason,
Where she wouldn't have persuaded
Pelias' girls to kill their father,
Nor be living here in Corinth
With her husband and her children,
Where her loyalty to Jason
Was so pleasing to its freemen,
Since a woman's safest conduct
Is agreement with her husband.

Closest friendships turn to hatred.
Deepest love is disregarded.
Jason's made a royal marriage
With the daughter of King Creon,
Who's the ruler of this country.

Poor Medea, scorned and slighted,
Shouts aloud his wedding pledges
And the solemn oaths he uttered;
Calls the gods to be her witness
How he's broken every promise.
Giving in to her emotions,
She lies fasting, she lies weeping.
All her day is passed in teardrops,
Since she learnt of her betrayal.

Eyes and face are firmly downcast.
Hears no more the consolation
Any friends may try to offer
Than a rock in choppy waters,
Saving when she twists her white neck
To bewail her dear old father,
Home and country she surrendered
For the man with whom she came here:
Since he's treated her so badly,
She has learnt through this disaster
Just how vital is your homeland.

Now alas she hates her children,
Has no pleasure when she sees them.
I'm afraid of what she's planning,
For she has a dreadful temper,
Cannot bear to suffer wrongly.

As I know her I'm suspecting
She will stab right through her stomach,
Having sneaked into the chamber,
Where the bridal bed is laid out,
Kill the king and then the bridegroom,
Taking chances on the outcome.
For she is a holy terror:
Take her on in any contest,
You'd be most hard put to beat her.

Enter children and elderly tutor from stage left.

From their running come the children.
Mother's problems-they're quite heedless-
For the young are always cheerful.

TUTOR   Old house servant of my mistress,
Should you pass time standing outside,
Going over your misfortunes?
Did she tell you, Go and leave me?

NURSE   Ancient minder serving Jason
As the tutor of his children,
You know how a master's problems
So affect their loyal servants

10

And attack their every feeling,
That I reached a peak of sorrow
I could not resist the longing
To speak out Medea's mishaps
To the sky and earth beneath us.

TUTOR   Has the wretch not ceased from moaning?

NURSE   It's your ignorance I envy,
For her grieving's just beginning.

TUTOR   Stupid, though I should not say that,
For she is my lady mistress,
But she faces further problems.

NURSE   What's that, old man? Kindly tell me.

TUTOR   No, it wasn't right to speak out.

NURSE   By your beard I surely beg you
To admit a fellow servant
Into secrets you're possessing.
You can trust me to keep silence.

TUTOR   Seeming to be out of earshot,
When I heard some people speaking
At the place for draughts and chequers,
Where the old men sit and idle,
By the sacred fount Peirene,
How King Creon had decided
That the children should be thrown out
With their mother from this country.
Whether this is true I know not.
I would rather hope it were not.

NURSE   Surely Jason would not let this
Suffering fall upon his children,
If there weren't a further dispute
He'd engaged in with their mother?

TUTOR   All gives way to his new marriage.
He's no longer friend to this house.

NURSE   Well then we're completely ruined,
             Adding new woes to the old ones,
             Old ones that we hadn't sorted.

TUTOR   Please keep quiet and say nothing.
             This would hardly be the right time
             To appraise your mistress of this.

NURSE   Poor dear children, did you hear this:
             How your father dares to treat you?
             Damn him, though I shouldn't say that,
             He's my master, but indicts him
             Bad behaviour to his loved ones.

TUTOR   It's a fact that we're all human.
             Long ago you must have learned this,
             How we fail to love our neighbour,
             Sometimes truly with good reason,
             Or just for the sake of profit,
             If he fails to love his children,
             All because of this new marriage.

NURSE   Let us hope that matters prosper.
             Children will you please go indoors.
             Steer them clear of their poor mother,
             While she's in this awful temper.
             Most of all do not go near her.
             I have seen her eye them madly,
             Quite prepared to do them evil.
             She will not give up her anger,
             Till she vents her spleen on someone.
             May it be a hostile person,
             Not upon her own dear children.

The tutor takes the children inside Medea's house.

MEDEA *from within*
             Misery, ruin, sorrow on sorrow.

NURSE   Children, children will you heed this:
             Mother's fully roused with anger
             In her heart and in her spirit.
             Run inside the house so swiftly.

Do not stray inside her vision.
Do not anyway approach her.
Guard against her wild passions.
Guard against her evil temper.
Guard against her wilful nature.
I repeat-go inside quickly.

Her initial clouds of anger
From the greater fires within her
Blaze with ever deeper fury.
Stung by all these sad misfortunes,
What she'll do I dare not think of,
When there's no check on her daring.

MEDEA *from within*
I cannot bear this, why should I suffer
Sufferings dire, sufferings painful?
Just let him perish, along with his children.
Cursed be they; I no longer love them;
Bring down the house; bring doom and
destruction.

NURSE   This pains me also. I too am wretched.
Why should they pay for the sins of their father?
Why do you hate them, poor little infants?
May it not happen what I am fearing.
For she's descended from absolute rulers.
That's why she has such a terrible temper:
Tyrannous, self-willed, knows no restraint.
Better and safer to live with your equals
Than to grow old with the high and the mighty.
We all need balance, we need moderation,
Earning a living in good honest toil.
What good is excess of money or power,
If when your luck turns you fall so much further?

CHORUS   Terrible screams come from Medea's house,
wretchedly--
She so unsoothed, unappeased sadly--
Piercing the chambers of my house distressfully.
Tell me the causes at least summarily.
Don't think that I'll hear misfortune happily.
For in this house I spent time pleasantly.

13

NURSE
When the house was a home, yes, so cheerfully.
Now alas it's broken up utterly:
He to his new wife gone so gladly,
Poor Medea, so upset totally,
Sobs and sulks and pines obsessively.

MEDEA
May lightning strike me.
What have I to live for?
My life is hateful.
Let death come quickly.

CHORUS
Heaven and earth must hear her death wish.
How mad to yearn for, or hasten our final rest.
Don't even think it, that is my message,
All for a husband who's broken his pledges.
Leave it to Zeus to make some amendment.

MEDEA
It's the daughter of Zeus who's defender of Justice.
Themis she's called. To her I make my prayers.
Guardian, steward and defender of oaths,
Look at the misery I suffer painfully,
All at the hands of one who swore solemnly.
Punish him ruthlessly,
Kill his wife savagely,
Here, where they wronged me with every
intention,
Who for him treated my father so shamelessly,
Who for him killed my own brother brutally.

NURSE
Listen to her, listen to her, listen to her carefully.
In calling for justice she calls for it vengefully,
Not for the ending of anger appeasingly.

CHORUS
If she approached the sound of our voices,
She might dismiss her desperate hard-heartedness.
Let's not abandon a friend when they need us.
Go bring her here, speak some encouragement,
Lest she resorts to an act of savagery,
Driven by grief to behave so irrationally.

NURSE
I will attempt it. I will try willingly.
Somehow I doubt I shall do it successfully.

When I last neared her, she snarled quite
ferociously.

You would be right to think our forefathers
Stupid and foolish: they invented musicals,
Songs for festivities, banquets and jollities;
But never found sounds which would chase off
depression,
Never found tunes to assuage human bitterness,
Never found chords to end the despair
Which poisons relationships, ruins establishments.
What a boon that would be, what a great cure all!
Why waste good music on revellers and gluttons?

Exit nurse into Medea's house.

CHORUS   I hear her moans, her lamentations.
Shrill her screams, her accusations,
In her prayer for retribution:
How he swore to true devotion,
So she crossed the vast deep Pontus,
Through the straits to Greece so freely,
Where he now treats her so badly,
Breaking vows he made so keenly.

Medea enters from her house with nurse and attendants.

MEDEA   Women living here in Corinth,
I've come out of doors with reason.
I don't want you to reproach me.
I know many are thought haughty,
Some for what they do in public,
Some for merely being private:
Others, who are quiet footed,
Are defamed for being idle.
Men's eyes really have no justice,
Hating someone just on first sight,
Not before they've learnt his nature,
Even when he hasn't wronged them.

Refugees should be compliant
To their city of asylum,
But I wouldn't praise a local

15

Having such pride in his swagger
He offends his fellow townsmen,
When displaying his uncouthness.
This disaster, unexpected,
Fell on my life and destroyed it.
I've lost all the joy of living,
And, my friends, I long for dying.
He, with whom affairs did prosper,
My man, proved to be most evil.
All that breathe with power of thinking-
We poor women are most wretched:
Husbands purchased with huge dowry
Will be masters of our body,
Adding pain to gross injustice.
In this is the greatest contest-
Get a bad man or a good one:
For divorce will not bring credit,
And we can't refuse the wedding.

When we come to different customs,
Different standards of behaviour,
How we need to be prophetic!
No one indoors taught this science
As to how we should best please him.

If our labours are successful,
And the yoke is not resented,
He lives with us in contentment,
And our life is one to envy.
But if not, to die is better.

If a man's fed up when indoors,
He goes out to ease his boredom,
Turning to some friend or other.
No such choice for us, however-
We're supposed to mind *his* interests.

Men say our life lacks the danger
That they face in playing soldiers,
When we're safely staying indoors;
But that's really sloppy thinking.
Let me stand three times with shield
Than to lie down once in labour.

Your affairs and mine are different.
You live here in this your city,
In the houses of your fathers,
Where you can enjoy your own life
In the fellowship of good friends.

I'm deserted, with no homeland,
By my husband, who insults me,
Snatched from foreign parts as booty,
Neither mother, brother, kinsman
For a haven from my problems.

So this favour I will beg you:
If the ways and means discovered
For my man to give requital
In respect of all these evils,
And the one who gave his daughter,
And the girl herself who married,
You will surely guard my secret.

Though a woman fears for most things,
Poor at war and sight of steel,
Yet when crossed in matrimony,
No one's nature is more bloody.

CHORUS   Rightly should your man be punished:
So for you I will keep silence.
That you grieve at your misfortunes
Does not give me cause to marvel.

Creon enters from stage left

But I see King Creon coming,
Who's the ruler of this country,
And brings message of new counsels.

CREON   Raging madly with your husband,
And so sullenly resentful,
You, Medea, have to go now
Into exile from this country,
Taking both your children with you.
No delay will be permitted.
I'm the umpire of this ruling.

17

	I will not be going homeward,
	Till I've thrown you from these borders.

MEDEA   Poor me, I'm completely ruined.
When my foes set out full sail,
And there is no easy landing
From my ship of dire troubles,
I shall speak, though suffering badly-
When you send me from this country,
Who's the cause? Please tell me, Creon.

CREON   I am, for I truly fear you,
And I'll not disguise my reasons.
You intend some dreadful mischief
To conduct against my daughter.
There are many indications
To this fear in contribution.
You are truly wise and learned
In the practice of the dark arts,
Full of grief for your ex-husband,
Whose embraces you're deprived of.
I have heard what you are threatening-
There are many that do tell me-
To commit some act so dreadful
To the one who gives his daughter
To be married in the wedding,
To the bride and to the bridegroom.
I must truly guard against this.
Far, far better is it, woman,
At this moment, if you hate me,
Than I should relent in softness
And have cause to groan much later.

MEDEA   Well and truly full of sorrow,
I have frequently observed it,
When you have great reputation,
How it harms you causing problems.
No one with an ounce of common
Ought to educate their children
Into being over clever.
First they're charged that they're time wasters,
Then they earn ill will and envy
From the ranks of common townsmen.

If you try to teach the stupid
Something new by way of learning,
You will be accounted useless.
None at all will think you clever.
If perchance considered better
Than those who are just pretentious,
None the less you're still offensive.
In this fate I'm also sharing.
For my learning some resent me:
Others merely think I'm idle,
Or I'm living in my own world
And aloof. So am I clever?
Do you fear me, lest I'll harm you?
I'll assure you- there's no need to.
In me there is no such purpose
To attack the royal family.
There is no way you have wronged me.
Give your daughter who you want to.
It's my husband that I'm hating.
There is sense in all your actions.
Your success I'm not begrudging.
Marry, and may matters prosper.
Only will you let me stay here.
Of my wrongs I'll now be silent,
Giving way to better counsels.

CREON   When I listen, you're persuasive,
But my instincts fear you're plotting.
Less than ever do I trust you.
When a man or woman's raging,
Self-protection is much easier
Than when taciturnly clever.
Go off forthwith, don't speak further,
For my mind is quite well made up,
And your skills are not sufficient
To ensure that you will stay here,
When you bear me so much ill will.

MEDEA   By your knees and new wed daughter.

CREON   Don't waste words: you'll not persuade me

MEDEA	So you'll send me into exile, Disregard my supplications.
CREON	Yes, because I'll not prefer you To the running of my kingdom.
MEDEA	How I miss my own dear country.
CREON	Second dearest to my children.
MEDEA	Lord, what evils for us mortals Can be brought by love's sweet passion.
CREON	That depends on circumstances.
MEDEA	Zeus, please don't omit to notice Who's to blame for all my evils.
CREON	Be off will you, stop time wasting, And divide me from my troubles.
MEDEA	They're my troubles. I don't want them.
CREON	Soon my servants will expel you.
MEDEA	Please, not this, I beg you, Creon.
CREON	You just seem to cause me problems.
MEDEA	Then I'll go, but here's my last plea.
CREON	Must you be so quite constraining, With your hand so tightly clinging?
MEDEA	Just allow me to stay one day, To decide where I shall go to, And support for my dear children, Since their father shows no interest Into making their arrangements. Pity them, for you're a father, And it's right that you show kindness. Exile doesn't give me problems: Them I weep for in disaster.

CREON   Least of all am I despotic,
        Through respect sustaining losses.
        Woman, though I am in error,
        I shall grant you what you're asking.
        Well and truly must I warn you,
        If the following day's sunrise
        Lights upon you and your children
        In the borders of this country,
        You will die; my word is spoken.
        If you must stay, stay this one day.
        In this short time you can't harm me
        In the ways that I am fearing.

Creon exits stage left.

CHORUS   Wretched Medea, drowning in sorrows,
        Where does this leave you?
        Where will you turn to,
        Seeking asylum,
        Needing a new home,
        Haven and refuge?

MEDEA   Everything's dire. Who can deny it?
        But you'd be wrong to think me defeated.
        Don't think the newly weds haven't got problems,
        Or the old king who set up the wedding.
        Do you think I would have soft-soaped him,
        If I weren't plotting, planning or scheming?
        Would I have begged him, clasping his fingers?

        He's so damn stupid, he could have foiled me,
        Wrecking my plans with instant expulsion.
        But he's allowed me to stay this one day,
        And to make corpses three of my enemies,
        Him and his daughter and her new husband.
        There are so many ways to dispatch them.
        What to try first, that's my dilemma!
        Should I burn down the bridal chamber,
        Or stick a sharp sword straight through her stomach,
        Secretly entering the room with the marriage bed?

But if I'm caught before it's successful,
I will be killed: I will be laughed at.
Easiest and best has to be poison-
My special subject, my special training.
But when they're dead, where shall I go to?
I need a host, asylum and refuge.
Who will provide this, who'll be my rescue?
In fact there's no one or not just quite yet.

So I ought to wait for just a short time,
Hoping I should find some sort of safe house,
For my escape, after my dark crime,
To be conducted in stealth and silence.

But if I'm forced out, into the open,
With no retreat, then I'll do it boldly;
I'll grasp the sword and cut them up surely.
I'll dare the deed; I'll face the penalty.

I swear by Hecate, my sovereign mistress,
Whom I most worship, my chosen helper,
Guardian of my shrine, my inner temple,
Those who break my heart have had their last
laugh.
Bitter and grievous will be their nuptials,
Bitter their marriage, as is my exile.

Well now Medea, search out your knowledge,
Every last recess, doing your planning.
Don't shrink from terror. What counts is boldness.
Look what you've suffered. Don't let them mock
you
With this alliance founded on their tricks,
When you're a princess, sprung from the sun god,
When you're a woman, when no code of honour,
Poses restraint on your mode of fighting.

CHORUS   Men's plans are all so very twisted,
When they lightly break their stern oaths,
Disregarding sacred pledges,
Just as if all streams flow backwards,
And all justice is perverted.

But they say that times are changing,
Bringing women's lives more glory,
Turning much malignant slander
To respect and adulation.

Ancient songs will cease defaming
Women, as if we're all faithless.
Lord Apollo, God of Music,
Never taught the lyre's secrets
To poor females, or we'd play back
To the lusty male voice choirs,
Though we'd need a very long time
For the hymns of common failings.

Truly mad with love you sailed
From your father's far off homestead;
Slid between the rocks that guard the
Entrance to the stormy Pontus.

Now in foreign territory,
Separated from your husband,
Who has held you in dishonour,
You are driven into exile.

Oaths and pledges have no meaning.
There's no shame throughout the Greek world.
Into thin air it has vanished.

Wretch, you have no family household
To escape to from your troubles,
While another royal princess
Ousts you from your home and husband.

Jason enters from stage left.

JASON   Insoluble problems are caused by bad temper,
Rifts of a kind that cannot be mended.
Time and again I've had to observe this:
For *you* had a home and place in this country,
Whilst you deferred to the whims of its rulers,
But got expelled for your silly grumbling.

23

Say what you like-*I* wasn't upset.
Evil man Jason, terrible monster,
But when you slandered those who hold power,
You were quite lucky just to be thrown out.
I tried to calm down their ruffled feathers,
So you could stay, but there was no chance.
You kept insulting all the blood royals.
You couldn't stop being so stupid.
So once again, that's why you're expelled.

Nevertheless I've not disowned you,
My former loved one; for I have come here,
Guarding your interests, though you are thrown
out,
Going to exile, with both our children,
Trying to make sure you'll still have money,
Knowing the problems that you'll be facing;
For though you hate me, I still respect you.

MEDEA   You utter bastard, how else to describe you,
Spineless and shameless, obscene little coward,
How can you come here, after what you've done,
Hateful to me, to God and all people?
When you've truly wronged your loved ones,
And you dare to stand and face them,
Is that courage, is that boldness,
Are you merely being cheeky?
Not at all, you're downright wicked,
Suffering from the worst of scourges,
That you're lacking shame and honour
In effrontery so brazen.

None the less I'm glad to see you,
For by giving you an earful,
Basting you with words so stinging,
When you start to feel sorry,
My morale will be uplifted.

So we'll start at the beginning
With the task you were allotted,
Sent to plant a crop so deadly,
Yoking bulls that breathed out fire,
When I saved you, as they know well,

24

Who came with you on the Argo.
When I killed the sinuous serpent,
Coiled and twisted round the gold fleece,
Guarding it and never sleeping.
When I held the torch of safety
For you and your fellow crewmen,

When I left my home and family
For a journey to Iolcus,
Far too eager, far too stupid,

When I killed your uncle Pelias
In a death so downright horrid,
At the hands of his own daughters,
So we could take over power.
And what thanks then am I getting
For these many, many favours
Done for you, you foul betrayer?

You've decided to divorce me,
And contract another marriage,
Though I've given you two children,
And it's only lack of offspring
Which excuse a second union.

You have broken oaths and pledges,
Made with every divine sanction,
Just as if the gods stopped ruling,
Giving way to other powers,
Which accede to your deceiving.

Vainly were we used by this man,
And our hopes were much mistaken,
When he swore and clutched our right hand,
Kneeling down to grasp our kneecaps.

Let's pretend we are still good friends,
And I'm wanting your opinion,
Though I doubt you'd do me much good,
But your failure counts against you,
Makes you so much more disgraceful.

Will you tell me where to turn to,
When you know that I have nowhere:
Can't go back home to my father,
Whom for your sake I mistreated,
Or the daughters of King Pelias,
Poor sad wretches, back in their home,
How on earth would they receive me,
Knowing how I killed their father?

Things are hostile on the home front,
Where I treated all so badly,
Though I really didn't need to
Turn them into foes so bitter,
Doing you so many favours.

At the same time most Greek women
Think my lot is so much better
Than the life that they are leading,
Just as if you were a byword
For a truly faithful husband,
When you've taken on a new wife!

What a fine start to a marriage,
That the groom's ex has been thrown out,
When it was the ex who saved you,
And she wanders homeless, friendless,
A lone beggar with her children!

Oh dear God, why did you give us
Proofs for checking gold from glitter,
But to tell us who's a bad man
There's no mark upon his body?

CHORUS   Truly awful is the anger,
          Causing ills that can't be healed,
          Consequent on marriage breakdown,
          And the strife which it engenders.

JASON   Your invective's like a gale,
          Blowing over stormy waters,
          When the skipper trims his sails,
          Flying downwind on the wave crest,
          And won't try to tack against it,

Lacking powers of counter speaking
To disprove your stupid charges
That your aid was so important,
When my saviour was the goddess
Aphrodite, known as Cypris.
She alone was my true helpmate.
Oh your thinking may be clever,
But the truth is quite unpleasant:
Cupid's dart was what compelled you.
Let us not precisely argue.
Your assistance was quite welcome.
But you got more than you gave me,
As I'll now proceed to tell you:
Here in Greece you dwell securely,
Where the rule of law is honoured,
Not in some barbarian fiefdom,
Where there's no restraint on power.
More than that, your reputation
For your skills in natural science
Spreads about throughout the Greek world.
Were you still in far off Colchis,
Who on earth would know about you?
What's the point of having riches,
Or the skill to sing like Orpheus,
If you're just an unknown person,
Lacking fame and adulation?

That's enough about my labours,
Which I didn't mean to mention,
In a silly verbal contest,
Which you started in your wisdom,
Slanging off my royal marriage.
First I'll show you why it's clever,
And it's prudent, in the interests
Of yourself and of the children.
When we came to here from Iolcus,
Being two asylum seekers,
Bringing many troubles with us,
What could be a better prospect
Than to wed the king's own daughter?
And it wasn't, though it grates you,
That I had gone off our love life,
Or was smitten with my new bride,

Or was wanting lots more children-
It was only done for money,
To improve our living standards.
For a poor man has so few friends,
And to raise our kids in style
Would be helped if they had brothers,
Who, though royals, were just equals,
And together we would prosper;
For my children of the future,
Whom I'd father on another,
Would so help our present offspring.
So why should you feel slighted?
You've no need to feel broody.
Must you so dislike my planning,
Just because you've lost your sex life?
That's what's giving you the needle:
In your woman's scheme of values
All that counts is conjugation,
So that when it's that you're lacking,
You don't value other matters
That are so much more important.

God, it really would be better
To have children without women;
For if mortals were all males,
We'd be free of every evil!

CHORUS   Jason, though you argue deftly,
              Though it is my own opinion,
              Yet I think you're acting wrongly
              In divorcing poor Medea.

MEDEA   Am I on a different planet
              From the mass of other mortals,
              When I say unjust behaviour
              Should be punished more severely,
              If the wrongful perpetrator
              Is himself a clever speaker,
              Who will cloak bad deeds with smart words,
              And then dare to do more evil?
              But his guile isn't foolproof.
              So don't give me all your flannel.
              I'll demolish every premise

28

	Of your so elaborate defence.
	If your motives were above board,
	What was wrong with consultation?
	Did you try to first persuade us,
	When you made your new engagement?

JASON   You would not have been receptive,
If I'd told you of the marriage,
As a mere advance proposal,
When, despite the time elapsing,
You just won't give up the anguish,
When you nurse it as a grievance.

MEDEA   That was really not your reason:
You just thought that in your old age
To be married to a migrant
Wouldn't bring good reputation.

JASON   Well and truly must you realise
How it wasn't for the woman
That I made this royal marriage,
But as I have said so often,
Saving you and our whole household,
By begetting royal infants
Of the half blood to our children.

MEDEA   Such good fortune would be bitter.
In my life let me avoid it;
It would truly tear my heart out.

JASON   If you wanted to seem wiser,
You should learn to say this new prayer,
That sane plans should not seem grievous,
And that when you have good fortune,
You should not account it bitter.

MEDEA   To say that is so insulting,
When it's you that has the refuge,
And it's me goes into exile.

JASON   It was you yourself who chose it.
So you cannot blame another.

MEDEA	Are these deeds then all my doing?
	Was it me who got remarried
	And divorced you so unfairly?

| JASON | But you made unholy curses, |
| | When you cursed the royal family. |

| MEDEA | And accursed to your household. |

JASON	More of this I will not argue:
	Tell me if you want assistance
	From my money for the children
	Or yourself, when off in exile.
	I will give with hand unstinting,
	To my contacts sending tokens,
	Who will help you to their utmost.
	Turn this down and you are stupid.
	Gain results by ceasing anger.

MEDEA	We would not apply to your friends,
	Nor would we accept things from them.
	Do not therefore give us tokens.
	Worthless are the gifts of bad men.

JASON	I must call the Gods to witness
	How I really want to help you
	And the children all I'm able.
	But my kindness doesn't please you.
	Thrust your friends off, being stubborn,
	Only multiplies your sorrows.

Exits stage left.

MEDEA	You now go; you're seized with longing
	For your new bride, whilst you're spending
	All this time outside the palace.
	Wed her, for perhaps, with God's help,
	Such a wedding will disown you.

CHORUS	When love's passion comes to excess,
	No way does it bring us mortals
	Any credit for great virtue.
	But when fancy's finely balanced,

No divinity is sweeter.
Goddess, do not fire your arrows
At me from your bow so golden,
Aimed so deadly, smeared with longing.
Sooner loose on me with passion
Firm control of my emotions,
Greatest gift the gods can offer.
Let not Cypris, when she's awful,
Send on me contentious yearnings,
Paired with quarrels never ending,
Smiting my soul with desire
For relations with a stranger,
But with clear head may she match make,
Reverencing peaceful union.

House and country, let me not be
Homeless stranger, all time weary,
All my problems no resolving,
All my sorrows to be pitied.
Let death seize me, let death seize me,
Ending that day, ere such mishap.
No worse troubles ever happen
Than to lose your native soil.

We have seen it, we have seen it,
Not from hearsay do we tell this;
As you suffer worst of evils,
There's no pity from your home town,
There's no pity from your loved ones.
May he perish disrespected
Who cannot so trust his loved ones
As to bear his own soul to them.
Such a friend I am not wanting.

Enter King Aegeus from stage right

AEGEUS   Medea, how I wish you joy,
For when we start to talk to friends,
Who knows a prelude quite so fine?

MEDEA   Aegeus, may you too rejoice,
O son of Pandion the wise,
Whence come you here unto this land?

AEGEUS	From Phoebus ancient shrine.
MEDEA	The earth's own true prophetic heart So tell me please, why went you there?
AEGEUS	To know how I should children sire.
MEDEA	Till now, by God, you're childless.
AEGEUS	No children by some act of God.
MEDEA	But tell me if you have a wife, Or marriage is to you unknown.
AEGEUS	To matrimony I am used.
MEDEA	Of offspring what did Phoebus say?
AEGEUS	Some words too wise for human ken.
MEDEA	But right for me to know those words?
AEGEUS	Oh yes, we're needing your wise mind.
MEDEA	So tell me if to hear is right.
AEGEUS	Do not unplug the wineskin's stop.
MEDEA	Before what's done or where is reached?
AEGEUS	Before I'm back to hearth and home.
MEDEA	So wanting what you sailed here?
AEGEUS	There is a man named Pittheus, The king of all Trozenians.
MEDEA	The son of Pelops, most revered.
AEGEUS	With whom I wished to share the word.
MEDEA	A man so wise in all these things.

AEGEUS	And dearest of my army pals.
MEDEA	So may you prosper and fare well.
AEGEUS	Your eye and skin suffused with tears?
MEDEA	The cause my husband, worst of men.
AEGEUS	What's that you're saying? Tell me more About the sorrows of your heart.
MEDEA	It's Jason who has done me wrong, But never did I give him cause.
AEGEUS	What has he done? Please tell me more.
MEDEA	He's wed a woman in my place, And made her mistress of my house.
AEGEUS	He never dared such dire deed?
MEDEA	Know truly that he really did, And so dishonoured his loved ones.
AEGEUS	So was he smitten with his bride, Or had he come to loathe your bed?
MEDEA	It truly was a passion grand That caused him to betray his kin.
AEGEUS	If he's as bad as so you say, Perhaps it's best to let him go.
MEDEA	He sought a bride of royal blood.
AEGEUS	Who gave her him? Please tell me that.
MEDEA	Creon, of course, the ruler here.
AEGEUS	I understand your bitterness.

MEDEA   I am destroyed, and what is more
                I'm to be driven from the land.

AEGEUS   By whom this further ill you speak?

MEDEA   Creon's the one who's driving me
                Exile from the land of Corinth.

AEGEUS   And you say that Jason lets him!
                Well for that I cannot praise him.

MEDEA   Not expressly he approves it,
                But endures with acquiescence.
                By your beard I truly beg you,
                By your knees I supplicate you,
                Pity, pity me so wretched.
                Do not see me banished, lonely.
                In your land and home receive me,
                As a guest beside your hearth stone.
                Then by God you will have children,
                As your sex life proves productive,
                And your life will end with fortune.
                Such a find in me is founded.
                I will end your lack of children:
                I will make you sire offspring.
                I have knowledge of the medicines.

AEGEUS   May you know that I do thank you
                Eagerly for many reasons,
                First of all religious duty,
                Then the children which you promise.
                But for this I am quite helpless.
                Here and now I state the problem.
                If you're coming to my country,
                As I'm just I'll try to help you,
                But beforehand I must warn you:
                From this land I will not take you.
                Come to my house by your own means:
                You will gain a safe asylum.
                I will give you up to no one.
                Make your way from out this country.
                In the eyes of those my hosts here
                All my actions should be blameless.

MEDEA   So it shall be: can you swear it?
           Then you really would best please me.

AEGEUS   You don't trust me? What's your problem?

MEDEA   Yes indeed I surely trust you,
           But oppose me royal households,
           Those of Pelias and Creon.
           If they sought to extradite me,
           You'd refuse, if bound by pledges;
           But an unsworn verbal promise
           Is too easy to relinquish
           As a friend to their entreaties.
           I am weak, but they are wealthy,
           Living in their royal houses.

AEGEUS   In your words you show much foresight.
           If you want it, then I'll do it.
           What for me is surely safest
           Lies in having some excuses
           For refusing your opponents,
           And for you it is securer.
           Name the gods that I should swear by.

MEDEA   By earth's soil, by the sun god-
           He's my very own grandfather-
           Swear by them and in addition
           Each last one of the immortals.

AEGEUS   What is it that I must swear to?

MEDEA   Never ever to expel me
           From your land; if someone hostile
           Wants to take me, to oppose them,
           While you live, with all your power.

AEGEUS   By the Earth I'm truly swearing,
           By the Sun God's holy power,
           And by every god and goddess,
           To the oath from you I'm hearing.

MEDEA   That suffices; now what happens
           If your oath should be dishonoured?

AEGEUS   All the tortures of the damned.

MEDEA   Go rejoicing. All is well done.
            Soon your city I'll be reaching,
            When I've done what I'm intending,
            When obtaining what I'm wanting.

                    Aegeus exits stage left.

CHORUS   May the lordly son of Maia,
            God who guards and guides the traveller,
            Bring you safely back to your home.
            Sticking to it, be successful
            In the purposes you came for,
            Since, Aegeus, in my judgement,
            You're a man both kind and noble.

MEDEA   By Zeus and by the Holy sunlight,
            And by Justice, Zeus's daughter,
            Now my friends we'll be victorious,
            As we reach our journey's ending.
            Now at last I have a true hope
            That my foes will pay their misdeeds:
            In my moment of great weakness,
            When my plans required refuge,
            This man came as my safe haven.
            He's the moorings we require,
            Coming to the town of Pallas,
            Coming to the walls of Athens.
            Now I'll tell you what I'm planning,
            But my words won't give you pleasure.
            I shall send a slave to Jason,
            Asking him to come and see me.
            Then I'll speak him softly, softly:
            There was sense in his arrangements:
            Good idea the royal marriage,
            Never minding our betrayal,
            Most expedient, soundly thought out.
            Then I'll beg this one concession
            That my children should remain here-
            Not that I would really leave them
            In this land that is so hostile,

36

Where my foes might then insult them-
But to kill the king's own daughter
By a ploy of deadly cunning.
I shall send them to the princess,
Gifts in hand they're bearing to her,
Begging not to flee the country:
Silken gown and golden chaplet,
Taken, placed upon her fair skin,
She and all who touch her perish,
For the gifts are smeared with poison.
Then in my account I'm pausing,
Much lamenting deeds thereafter,
For I'm going to kill my children.
None of them will be exempted.
Having ruined Jason's household,
Then I'm going to leave the country,
Fleeing as a child murderess,
Having dared a deed unholy.
For, my friends, I'll not endure it
That my enemies should mock me.

This way, that way does it matter,
What's the point that's left in living?
Neither do I have a country,
Nor a home retreat from troubles.
How I really was mistaken,
When I left my father's household,
Trusting in a Greek man's promise,
Who by God will now be punished.
Children which on me he sired
He'll not see them; they're no longer;
Nor will he beget some others
On his newly wedded princess,
Since she's got to die quite awfully
By the agent of my poisons.
None should ever disrespect me,
Weak and feeble, easy picking,
When my temper's other styled,
Fierce on foes, but kind to loved ones,
Wherein lies true reputation.

CHORUS   Though with us you've shared your counsel,
           Yet because we want to help you,

	And support the laws we live by,
	Strictly tell you not to do this.
MEDEA	I cannot avert my action,
	Though I understand your thinking,
	But you haven't shared my sorrows.
CHORUS	Woman, can you kill your children?
MEDEA	It's the way to kill my husband.
CHORUS	It's the way to give you torture.
MEDEA	Then so be it. Words are surplus.

Addressing the Nurse

Will you go and bring me Jason.
For we use you as a trustee.
My intentions please keep quiet,
If you well respect your mistress,
If you truly are a woman.

Exit nurse stage left.

CHORUS   From immortal gods descended,
Blest of old the Erechtheids,
From a holy land unconquered,
Nurtured on most famous wisdom,
Gliding through the shining aether
On the Pierian Mountain,
Where they say that flaxen Concord
Gave birth to the nine pure Muses.

On Cephisus the streams flow clearly,
Where they say Cypris drew water,
Breathing on the land so sweetly
Temperate and pleasant breezes.
On her curls a crown she places
Made of rosy flowers fragrant,
Sending Love along with Wisdom,
Workers in all skills artistic.

How on earth then should this city,
Through which run the sacred rivers,
And which bears at each fiesta
All its gods in high procession,
How on earth should take in refuge
Someone who's to live among them,
Someone who has killed their children
Someone who is so unholy?

Will you think of what you're doing,
Wicked murder undertaking?
By your knees we supplicate you,
Absolutely, absolutely,
Not to murder your own offspring.

Whence then will you find the daring,
Dire boldness in your heartstrings
To lay hands upon your infants?
Can you cast your eyes upon them,
Tearlessly reflect their murder,
Plan that fate? Oh no you cannot,
When your babes fall down and beg you,
Wet your hand with their own bloodstains,
Driven by demonic passion.

Enter Jason from stage left with attendants.

JASON   I have come just as you asked me.
Even though you really hate me,
You will find me quite reliant.
What you want please kindly tell me.
Surely know that I will listen.

MEDEA   It's your pardon I am begging
For the former words I've spoken.
You should put up with my tantrums,
Since we used to share great passion.
I've gone over all my sayings,
Figured that I need a scolding,
Silly girl to be so raving,
Ill disposed to those who plan well,
Hostile to this country's rulers,
Bellicose towards my husband,

39

Who for me did what's expedient,
Contracting a royal marriage,
And begetting royal offspring
Of the half blood to my infants.
Can I not dismiss my anger?
What's my problem? God provides well.
I must think about my children.
We'll need friends, when fleeing this land.
Grasping this, I truly realised
Just how stupid was my reason,
Just how pointless was my anger.
Now at last I truly praise you.
Now at last your sense I realise
In contracting this new marriage.
I'm the one who's really senseless.
In your plans I should be sharing:
To your marriage lend assistance;
In attendance at your nuptials,
Look with pleasure on your new bride.
But we women will be women.
I should not defame us further.
So you should not share such evils,
Fending folly off with folly,
All my attitudes repenting,
I've resigned malicious thinking,
Having taken better counsels.
Children, children, please come hither,
Leave the house and come on outside,
Greet your father, who's here with us,
With your mother cease the warfare
We've engaged in with our dearest.
Anger's gone, we're reconciled.

The two boys come out of the house with the tutor.

Will you take him by the right hand.
Oh alas, for evils hidden.
Children, will you hold your palms out,
Even though you live a long time.
Wretched me, that am so tearful,
Wretched me, that am so fearful,
Now the former quarrel's ended,
That my sight's with teardrops clouded.

CHORUS   My eyes too with tears suffuse,
           Lest our troubles worse becoming.

JASON   For this I praise you now, good woman,
           And what's past I don't reproach you.
           For your sex to get so angry,
           If your husband takes a new wife
           All in secret, stands to reason.
           Though it's taken quite a fair time,
           Yet at last your view is changing,
           Recognising better counsel,
           Marking you a prudent woman.

           Great concern I've put, my children,
           To the question of your future:
           With God's help to make it certain.
           For I'm hoping, not before long,
           In the upper ranks of Corinth
           With your siblings you'll be counted.
           Only first you must reach manhood.
           All the rest will be accomplished
           By your father and by favour
           Of some well disposed immortal.
           How I hope to see you sturdy,
           When you reach the end of boyhood,
           Overcoming my opponents.

           Medea, why is it you're wetting
           Both your eyes with pale teardrops,
           Turning sideways with your white cheeks,
           Quite disheartened by my speaking?

MEDEA   Take no notice, it was nothing,
           Contemplating both our children.

JASON   Cheer up. I've provided for them.

MEDEA   Trusting in your words, I'll do that.
           Weak are women, prone to weeping.

JASON   What's the need to shed tears for them?

MEDEA   I'm their mother, I who bore them.
When you prayed for their own future,
I felt pity for what should be.
But the reason why you came here,
And the things I meant to tell you,
Some's been said, the rest I'll mention.
Since the rulers must expel me-
I admit it's right and proper-
Not to live and be in your way
Or the country's royal powers,
Since I'm bound to be resentful-
I shall sail into exile;
But so you should raise the children,
Beg King Creon let them stay here.

JASON   I don't think I can persuade him,
But I'll try to do my utmost.

MEDEA   Tell your wife to beg her father
That your sons don't leave the country.

JASON   Most of all I should persuade her.

MEDEA   If she is like other women.
In this task I will assist you.
I shall send her gifts the finest,
I know mankind has to offer,
Silken gown and golden chaplet,
Brought to her by our own children.
Quickly, quickly may a servant
Bring the dress and headband hither.

An attendant must leave at this point.

Not just once, but time and often,
She'll be gladdened to receive these
All from you, her noblest husband,
Gaining garments which the Sun God,
My grandfather, gave his children.

Enter attendants bearing poisoned robe and headband.

Take these bridal gifts, my infants,
Bear and give them to the princess,
Lucky bride to be receiving
Presents which are least shameworthy.

JASON   You can't part with these. It's foolish.
Do you think the royal palace
Wants for dresses and for gold work?
You must keep them; do not give them.
If she honours me, then truly
She'll prefer my plea to riches.

MEDEA   Don't deflect me, for I've been told
Gifts are known to bribe immortals.
As for humans gold is better
Than a million, million speeches.
She is queen and her's the hour.
Fate and fortune shine upon her.
To avert my children's exile,
Not just gold I'd give my own life.

Well then, children, go and enter,
The rich palace of your father,
Beg his new bride, beg my mistress,
Not to have to flee the country,
Give the outfit, most important,
To her hands direct in person.
Quickly, quickly, do the task well,
Then to mother bear glad tidings
What she wants is going to happen.

Jason, attendants, children and Tutor exeunt stage left.

CHORUS   Now quite truly, hope has left me
For deliverance of the children.
Off they go to certain murder.
When the bride receives the headband,
Wrought from beaten gold the finest,
She poor wretch receives destruction.
On her golden hair she places
With her own hands deathly headwear.
On her curls she'll put the chaplet,
By its heavenly charm persuaded,

43

And the garment's golden glitter.
To be bride of death she's dressing,
Into what a trap she's falling,
Doomed to death, alas so wretched,
And she won't escape her sad fate.

Wretched mother of doomed children,
How I weep for your misfortunes,
Which should make you kill your offspring.
Left deserted by your husband,
Breaking all his sacred pledges,
For the sake of this new marriage,
For the sake of his new partner.

Enter Tutor stage left.

TUTOR   Oh my mistress, I've some good news:
Cancelled is your children's exile,
For the princess with much gladness
In her hands received the presents.
There's peace henceforth for your offspring.
Why stand shocked about your fortune,
Turned aside, so what's your reason?
Aren't you thrilled to hear this message?

MEDEA   Alas.

TUTOR   At odds with my announcement.

MEDEA   And again alas.

TUTOR   Some mishap
In my message? I'm mistaken
That it's good news, when it isn't.

MEDEA   I'm not blaming your announcement.
You have told us what you told us.

TUTOR   Why so downcast then and weeping?

MEDEA   Old man, it's with much good reason.
Things I've planned through my own madness-
Me and my gods wrongly thinking.

TUTOR   There's no need to be disheartened.
                One day you'll come back from exile
                By the will of your own children.

MEDEA   But I'll bring them home before then.

TUTOR   You alas are not the first one
                To be parted from your children.
                Sufferings go with being mortal,
                So we ought to bear them lightly.

MEDEA   I will do so. Now go inside.
                Children's daily bread prepare them.

Tutor exits into Medea's house.

Oh my babies, oh my babies,
In this town that's now your hometown,
Parted from your wretched mother,
You will live and never see her.
To another land I'm going,
Exiled where I can't enjoy you,
Nor will watch you grow and prosper,
Will not dress your future spouses,
Wedding bed or hold up torches.
Insane boldness is my ruin.
Vainly, children, did I rear you,
Vainly worked, constrained in labours.
Once I had such great hopes for you,
Caring for me in my old age,
When I'd gone my body wrapping,
Family life's ideal picture.
Gone is now that rosy prospect.
Without you a life of sorrow,
Pain and grief is what I'm leading.
Love in eyes, you won't see mother,
To your future life departing.

Alas, dear children, staring, asking
Why it is you so regard me,
Why you make that final smile?
What to do, my will has faltered,
Women, when I saw their bright eyes?

45

I can't do it. Plans are cancelled.
I shall take them into exile.
Should I double my own troubles,
When I'm stinging their own father
With their slice of new misfortune?
No, of course not, plans are cancelled.

What's my problem? I'll be laughed at,
If my foes should go unpunished.
I must do it. I must do it.
Not let sentiment dissuade me.

Go inside the house, dear children.

The children go inside the house.

At this sacrifice I'm making,
If your instincts are offended,
To your own concern be looking.
I will not withhold my action.

No, Medea, don't you do it,
Sad one, leave them, spare your infants,
Let them live with us and please us.

No, by all the darkest powers
Down in Hell, it never shall be
I'd permit our foes so hostile
To insult my dearest children.
Die they have to, die they must do,
I who bore them, I should kill them,
No avoidance, has to be done.

Now the crown's been put on her head,
So the bride and royal princess
Dies inside her wedding garment.
This I realise all too clearly.
Taking now a bitter journey,
Sending them on one that's more so,
I must speak to both my infants.
Children, children come to mother,

The children enter on stage from the house.

46

Holding out your tiny right hands,
Children with your hands so lovely,
Children with your mouths so sweet,
With your form and visage noble,
Prosper there, not here, where rather
Father took away your future.
Children, with your tender kisses,
Children, with your skin the softest,
Children, with your breath the sweetest.
Go then go. I'll not behold you,
Any more your present format,
Worsted so by all that's evil.

The children exit and go back into the house.

What I'm doing, though I know it,
That it's wicked, I can't help it;
For my passion's so much greater
Than my self control and reason;
That's what causes for us mortals
Far the most amount of evil.

Medea exits stage left.

CHORUS   Conversations so much finer,
And contentions so much rarer,
Than we women should engage in
I have often been involved in,
Inasmuch we have our own muse,
Calling when some wisdom's needed.
Not on all-the class is tiny,
Hardly found among so many
Unto whom the muse is given.
By that muse that I am saying
Anyone who's not had children's
Lot is better than a parent's.
With no children then you don't know
Whether they bring pain or pleasure,
So by that you're kept from sorrows,
Sorrows that you don't encounter
In your house, when blessed with offspring.
How I see you all time worn out,
Caring firstly for their raising,

And on death to leave them something,
Whether labours should prove wasted,
Spent on wasters, that is unknown,
Or on those who should prove worthy.
Lastly telling of an evil
That for humans is the worst one,
When they find the means to raise them,
And they've grown from youth to manhood,
Children that you're rightly proud of,
But because of some god's purpose
Early death to Hades takes them,
Luckless bodies of your children.
How on earth then does it profit,
When the Gods impose on mortals,
For the sake of having children,
This most grievous painful passion,
Adding to all other troubles?

Medea enters stage left.

MEDEA   The event I'm long awaiting,
And its outcome I'm expecting,
Friends, we are about to hear of;
For I'm seeing Jason's servant
Coming, but by his forced breathing
Seems to show bad news he's bringing

Enter Messenger from stage left.

MESSENGER   From your deed so black and lawless
You, Medea, have to go now,
Land or sea this very instant,
Taking boat or coach or carriage.

MEDEA   Will you tell me what has happened
As a reason for my leaving?

MESSENGER   Both have perished by your poisons,
Royal princess and her father,
Old King Creon, just this instant.

MEDEA   That's the finest word you've spoken-
Friend henceforth and benefactor.

MESSENGER   What is this I hear you saying-
             Comes from mad and crooked thinking-
             When you've so outraged their household,
             That you hear it with rejoicing,
             With no fear of royal vengeance?

MEDEA   I assure you I have something
             As an answer to your statements.
             In the meantime don't be hasty.
             Tell me, tell me how they perished.
             Truly my delight is doubled,
             Hearing how they died so awfully.

MESSENGER   Your twins coming with their father
             Right inside the bridal chamber,
             All we servants were delighted.
             We had felt for all your problems.
             To the news our ears were buzzing.
             Your and Jason's quarrel settled.
             One of us their hand was kissing,
             One of us their blonde hair stroking.
             With this joy, the rules forgetting,
             To the women's chambers followed
             With the children I who shouldn't.
             There the mistress, now in your place,
             Whom we honour, give respect to,
             All her eyes were fixed on Jason,
             Till the entrance of your children,
             When she shuts them up completely,
             Turns aside her high white cheekbone,
             Quite disgusted at their coming.
             But your husband's then removing
             Bile and temper of his new bride,
             Saying, "Don't despise my loved ones,
             Cease your rage and turn your head back.
             Count them also your own darlings,
             Just as they are to your husband.
             Take the gifts, beseech your father,
             To remit the children's exile,
             Do it please, a favour to me."
             But then once she saw the costume,
             No way could she then be held back,
             Granting all her husband's asking.

Father, children hadn't gone far
From the chambers after leaving,
When she took the fine weave garment,
Placed the gold crown on her tresses,
Combing hair in front of mirror,
Smiling at her lifeless image.
Rising then from where she's seated,
Goes and walks the women's quarters,
Pointing nicely with her white feet,
With her presents so delighted.
Over and again she's looking
At the straightness of her sinews.
Then alas a dire wonder:
Changes colour, staggers backward,
Limbs a tremble, just stops falling
To the ground, on chair she's landing.
Then one of the ancient servants,
Thinking this a fit inspired,
Brought by Pan or other being,
Shouts with joy, until she's seeing
From her mouth white foam is coming,
Pupils in her eyes are twisting,
And her skin's a deathly pallor.
Then an awful scream she's uttered,
In a strain so very different.
One goes rushing to her father,
And another to her husband,
Telling of the bride's undoing.
So the chambers are resounding
With the noise of rapid running.

In the time a race course sprinter
Can complete his second half lap
She, unhappy girl, is rousing
From her dumb and sightless coma,
Making first an awful groaning,
When a second woe attacks her,
As the gold crown set on her head,
Truly an unholy wonder,
Bursts into a flame of fire,
All consuming in its power,
And the finely woven garment,
Given by your dearest children,

50

To this sad unhappy princess,
Eats the flesh from off her body.
Standing from the chair all flaming,
Running wants to hurl the crown off,
Shaking hair and head in all ways,
But the gold it keeps its fastenings
Far too fixedly and firmly.
When she shakes her hair, the fire
Just keeps burning more than ever.
To the floor she falls collapsing,
By this dire deed defeated.
You would hardly recognise her,
If you hadn't been her parent.
First her eyes have lost formation,
Next her face has lost its features.
Blood that's spurting out of her head
Is reacting with the fire.
From her bones her flesh is melting,
Just as is it were pine resin
By these hidden jaws of poison.
Never saw I sight so awful.
None of us would dare to touch her,
For her fate was our exemplar.
But her sad and wretched father,
Knowing naught of this disaster,
Comes into the room and straightway
Stumbles on her, greatly shrieking,
Clasps her in his arms to kiss her,
Asking his unhappy daughter
Which immortal has destroyed her,
In this way bereft of honour,
Turning him into a tombstone,
"As an old man sadly orphaned.
I should die with you my child."

When he stops his cries and groaning,
Tries to raise his aged body,
Finds he sticks to her like ivy
Clings around a laurel's branches:
So the garment tightly grips him
In the most unholy struggle,
As he tries to lift himself up,
But he's glued and bonded to her.

When with force he tries to free him,
Old man's flesh from bones is tearing.
Time's now short, his life is quenching,
Lucklessly his last is breathing,
Overcome by this disaster.
Lie the corpses close together
Daughter and her aged father.
All should weep for their misfortune.
But your prospects I can't speak of.
You could hardly go unpunished.

Life is just a fleeting shadow-
Not the first time I have thought this.
Don't be frightened, when I'm saying
That the wisest looking people,
Those who seem to know the answers,
They're the ones that I find fault with.
Man's estate is hardly lucky.
One who's richer than another
May be said to better prosper
Doesn't mean his God is kinder.

Exits stage left.

CHORUS   Jason well deserves the sorrows
Fate has sent him on this one day,
But the daughter of King Creon
How we mourn her sad misfortune.
She poor wretch to Hades travels,
Thanks to her mistaken marriage.

MEDEA   My dear friends, the deed's decided:
With great haste to kill my children
And then straightway leave the country.
If I wait for just a moment,
Someone else will surely seize them
For a murder far more bloody.
Die they must do, there's no option,
So in that case I should kill them,
I who bore them, let it be so.
Steel yourself and do not falter.
Though it's evil, but it's destined.
Take the sword, accursed right hand,

Though your after life be wretched.
Don't be weak and don't be feeble,
All because you loved your babies.
For this brief spell just forget it.
Grieve hereafter. Though you killed them,
Didn't mean you never loved them.
Only that your fate's against you.

Medea rushes inside the house.

CHORUS   On earth I kneel and pray the sun god.
With your rays that dazzle brightly
Look upon this hell bent woman,
With her own hand set on killing
Her own flesh, her own dear children.
From your golden birth she's seeded:
So their blood is part immortal:
And more fearful is its shedding.
Light of wonder, will you stop her,
From this house keep out the fury
Which incites the serial killer.

Through the dark grey razor sharp rocks,
Straits that guard the stormy Pontus,
That was how she came to Hellas,
Where she's wasted all her efforts
Giving birth to little children,
Wasted all love's tender feelings.

Wretched woman, what mad anger
So assaults your mind and reason
That you'd stoop to bloody murder
For the sake of stupid vengeance?

Kindred murder is so awful,
Tainting all in its pollution,
When the gods are sending earthward
On the kindred killer's homestead
Guilt that tortures and torments them.

CHILDREN   No please mother, do not do it.

CHORUS	Do you hear the screams of children,
	Locked up with that ill starred woman?
CHILD ONE	What shall we do, what shall we do,
	Where shall we flee the hands of our mother?
CHILD TWO	Oh my brother, that I know not,
	Truly brother we must perish.
CHORUS	Shall we go into the household?
	Shall we try to stop the murder?
CHILDREN	Yes, by God, please try to stop it.
	Yes, because it's right and needful.
	Yes, because the sword's upon us.
CHORUS	Truly, truly, wretched woman,
	With less heart than flint or granite,
	Shed your very children's' life blood,
	Disregarding that you bore them?
	Legends tell us of one woman
	Turned her hand against her children:
	Frenzied Ino, who was picked on
	By the wife of Zeus, named Hera.
	Sent abroad to wander madly,
	Killed her babes when on the cliff tops;
	Clutched them, jumping in the water;
	Perished in the sea together.
	What is worse than that we're asking?
	Pangs of birth we women labour
	Just brings troubles to us mortals!

Enter Jason and attendants.

JASON	Women standing near these chambers,
	Is Medea in the house still,
	Having done such wicked actions,
	Or made good a flight so rapid;
	For her choice is to be hidden
	Under earth or else fly upward,
	If she's not to pay the Royals
	Such requital they're demanding?

Did she think she'd kill the monarch,
Then escape as if not guilty?
But for her I'm not so bothered:
It's the children make me worry.
Let them punish her, they're welcome,
But I want to save my children,
Lest the royal close relations
For their mother's wicked murders
Want the blood of her own children,
In avenging expiation.

CHORUS Wretched Jason, how you know not
To what pitch of woes you've come to.
Had you known, you'd not have spoken.

JASON What is it?-To kill me also.
Is that what she's also wanting?

CHORUS I'm afraid she's killed the children.

JASON Alas, alas what are you saying?
How that woman has destroyed me!

CHORUS That they are alive no longer-
That's the fact you must consider.

JASON Where then was it that she killed them?
Was it in the house or elsewhere?

CHORUS Open up, behold their murder.

JASON At the double, come attendants,
Doors unbolt, put keys in deadlocks,
So I'll see the twofold evil,
Children dead and she who killed them-
For this deed she must be punished.

*Medea appears above the house in a chariot drawn by dragons.
In her arms she bears the dead bodies of her children.*

55

MEDEA   Can you tell me why you're moving
          Both the gates? -Is it to see me
          And the murders I've committed?
          You should cease this pointless labour.
          What you need to know please ask me.
          With your hands you'll never touch me,
          For the Sun God, my grandfather's,
          Given me this flying carriage
          For defence from all opponents.

JASON   You are such abomination,
          Greatest foe to all immortals
          And to every race of people
          And to me: you bore us children,
          Dared to kill them with a dagger,
          To destroy me in their losing.
          Having done this deed so awful,
          Crime by man and god detested,
          Show your face to earth and sunlight.
          Damn you, damn you, now I know it,
          Now I know it, then I didn't,
          When it was to Greece I brought you,
          From your foreign land and homestead,
          Who betrayed your native country
          And your father-he who raised you-
          How that was the greatest evil.
          But the god's on me inflicting
          Vengeance for your crimes so awful.

          When you slew your own dear brother
          To alight the ship of Argo,
          With its prow so nobly fashioned,
          That's the point from where I'm starting:
          When we first commenced our marriage,
          And you bore me two fine children,
          Whom you killed for slighted passion:
          No Greek woman ever dared this,
          Though I spurned them when I wed you.
          What a truly awful marriage,
          Partnered to a savage tigress,
          Fiercer far than any monster.

Go to Hell, you loathsome dealer,
You who dare to kill your children.
I'll lament my fate and downfall,
Nothing gained from my new marriage,
Nor the children whom I fathered
Raised and brought up to see living.
I am just destroyed completely.

MEDEA   In reply for quite a long time
I could match the words you've spoken.
But I really have no need to.
Father Zeus is understanding:
How I helped you in your labours,
How you treated all my favours.
Did you think your plan would prosper:
Throw me out for your new marriage,
Live a life of greatest pleasure,
Making jokes at my misfortunes?
Neither should the royal princess,
Nor the king who gave her to you,
Throw me from this land unpunished.
You can call me savage tigress.
Call me any kind of monster.
It's *your* heart that has been broken.

JASON   But you truly must grieve also,
Sharing in this pain and anguish.

MEDEA   Nothing means this pain and anguish,
If it stops you laughing at me.

JASON   Children, children, luckless were you
To be born of evil mother.

MEDEA   Children, children, what you died for
Was your father's moral sickness.

JASON   But it wasn't by my right hand
They received their fatal stabbing.

MEDEA   It was by your pride so wilful
In contracting this new marriage.

JASON	For this marriage was it lawful That you should resort to kill them?
MEDEA	When a woman is so slighted, Is it just a minor grievance?
JASON	If she's cool and level headed, But you see things in the worst light.
MEDEA	They're no more and that will hurt you.
JASON	Truly they will rise to haunt you.
MEDEA	When the gods know who begun this.
JASON	Someone with a mind so loathsome.
MEDEA	You may well reproach and hate me. How I hate your bitter mouthing.
JASON	Me too also, makes it easy At this last and final parting.
MEDEA	Really, what on earth shall I do, Also wanting separation?
JASON	Let me bury these my babies. Let me weep for these my children.
MEDEA	No way, no way: *I* will do that: With my own hand shall inter them At the temple in Acraea, Sacred to the goddess Hera, Lest my foes should desecrate them, Digging up their tiny coffins. As atonement for this murder- Yes I do admit it wicked- We shall start a sacred ritual Right here in the land of Corinth, Year by year without exception.

I am going off to Athens,
As a guest of King Aegeus.
As for you, it's only fitting,
As a scoundrel, to die basely
By a rotten plank of Argo,
Crashing on your skull and forehead,
You, who planned to end our marriage
In despite of my hurt feelings.

JASON   But it's you who will be haunted
For the murder of your children
By the furies and by Justice.
How I pray they will destroy you.

MEDEA   But what god or what immortal's
Like to hear the prayers you offer,
You who swore your oaths so falsely,
Disregarding obligations
To a foreigner who helped you?

JASON   Go to exile, child murderess.

MEDEA   Go back home, your wife to bury.

JASON   Home indeed, bereft of children.

MEDEA   You have hardly started mourning.
When you're old, it's then you'll miss them.

JASON   But you killed them. So how could you?

MEDEA   It was just to cause you anguish.

JASON   Anguished, anguished, well and truly,
Let me kiss my poor dead children.

MEDEA   First you didn't want to know them.
Now you want to bid them welcome.

JASON   By the gods please kindly let me
Touch the sweet skin of my children.

MEDEA   No, no, no your words are wasted.

JASON   Hear this Zeus, how she repels me,
                      What I've suffered from this tigress,
                      Loathsome, wicked child killer.
                      But with all my strength I'm crying,
                      Summoning the gods to witness.
                      First of all she kills my children,
                      Then she doesn't let me touch them,
                      Or to bury their dead bodies.
                      Would that I had not begat them,
                      Seen them slain by their own mother.

CHORUS   From the top of Mount Olympus
                      Father Zeus our fate's deciding.
                      Much will happen unexpected,
                      When the gods are intervening.
                      What we planned for doesn't work out.
                      By the hands of the Immortal
                      Comes to pass what least we hoped for.
                      That's the story we've just told you.

THE END

INTRODUCTION TO THE ALCESTIS OF EURIPIDES

Admetus, King of Pherae in Thessaly Ancient Greece, (on a modern map you'll find it close to Volos) has been fated to die young. But when Death comes to take his soul off to the underworld, it so happens that the god Apollo is temporarily working for him as a herdsman. Anxious to help his employer, Apollo comes to a bargain with the three Fates whereby Admetus can live the rest of his life out after all, if he can only find a substitute willing to die in his place. Admetus asks his elderly parents if they'll oblige, but they refuse. His friends aren't too keen on the idea either. In fact, the only substitute he can find is his wife Alcestis, and faced with losing her, he's beginning to wish the bargain had never been struck.

The play opens with the entrance of the god Apollo, dressed in a tunic and with his trademark bow and arrows on his back. He explains how he's been sent to earth as a herdsman: a punishment resulting from a rather murderous argument with his father Zeus the chief god. (Apollo's son Asclepius, the legendary discoverer of medicine and first physician, was killed by Zeus with a thunderbolt, lest the human race should become immortal, and in turn Apollo killed the Cyclops, the sons of Zeus who make thunder.) Apollo makes the introduction and then Death enters to claim the soul of Alcestis. She has been slowly wasting away and is expected to die at any moment.

Apollo and Death have an argument. Death suspects Apollo is going to trick him a second time and tells him to keep clear. However, Apollo hints that a man will come to the house and seize Alcestis from Death's hands. They both leave the stage and then the chorus discuss events. Greek plays always had a chorus on stage throughout the play, who would sometimes address the actors and at other times comment on events. Their commentaries would have been sung in ancient Greek times, but as we do not know the music that was used, the normal practise is for their lines to be collectively recited as spoken verse, sub-dividing the chorus as appropriate. Has Alcestis died or not? That's their big question. Alcestis' servant then enters. Alcestis is still alive, but only just, and knowing that her time has come, has said her prayers, dressed herself for the funeral and said goodbye to the servants. After further comment by the chorus, Admetus and Alcestis and their two children both come on stage to say their tearful farewells. Before dying, Alcestis makes Admetus promise he will never re-marry, and he pledges himself to do this. Alcestis fears that a new wife would only be a wicked stepmother to their children. She dies, and then there is much tearful commentary by Admetus, chorus and the children.

At this point, just as mourning has been ordered through out the land, Heracles arrives. He's more commonly known as Hercules, and is another son of Zeus. But as his mother Alcmene was a mortal, Heracles himself is also only mortal. However, he has fantastic strength, and is on his way to carry out one of his 12 famous labours, the capture and yoking of two man-eating mares. Admetus is now in a dilemma, because he feels it would violate the laws of hospitality if he should refuse to entertain his friend Heracles. He does not want him to go elsewhere, so resorts to the subterfuge that the mourning is for an orphan, no relation, who was taken in by the household. Heracles is then shown to the guest quarters of the palace.

The coffin is now brought on stage, and at this point Admetus's father, Pheres, and mother enter. They're bringing funeral gifts and Pheres praises Alcestis' noble sacrifice. Admetus is not at all pleased to see them. "You're already old," he says. "Why couldn't you have died for me? Then I could have lived out my life with Alcestis." Pheres does not agree. There's no tradition of fathers dying for their children, and life is sweet at any age. They have a blazing argument and all leave the stage, as does the funeral cortege.

Then a servant enters to complain about the behaviour of the guest Heracles. Here we are absolutely grief stricken and we've got to wait on this drunken oaf of a guest, as if nothing had happened! Heracles comes on to tell the servant off for being such a sour face and then learns the truth. "Where is the coffin to be interred?" he asks the servant, and discovers it's just outside the city. He then vows he will either ambush Death to recover Alcestis' soul, or else go down into the underworld itself to beg Hades, the god and king of the underworld, to release Alcestis' soul back to the daylight.

Heracles goes off and Admetus comes back on stage to discuss his grief with the chorus, until Heracles returns. What a strange story he has to tell! He's won a woman as a prize in a boxing match. He wants Admetus to look after this woman for him until he returns from capturing the savage mares. Although the woman is veiled, she's the same shape and size as Alcestis. "Please take her away," says Admetus, "I'm sworn never to touch another woman. What if I fell in love with her?" But Heracles is persistent and forces Admetus to hold her and to look at her. Yes, it's Alcestis, brought back from the dead. But she cannot yet speak to him, until the third day from when she was committed to the underworld, as for the moment she is still consecrated to the gods below. Admetus asks Heracles to stay on longer as his guest, but he says he must be on his way. And that concludes the play.

What do we make of it? Is it just a rather silly "tear jerker" with a happy ending, or is it a bit tongue in cheek? What do we make of Alcestis' death bed speeches? Are they credible? Does she secretly relish making Admetus feel so guilty? And in our present age, when we're all living longer and longer, isn't there a contemporary ring to the argument between Admetus and his father Pheres? If you were directing the play would you dare to have Pheres come on stage with a Zimmer frame and attached to a catheter? What does the play tell us about ancient Greek religion and its beliefs on death? What do we learn about funeral practices and the life in a nobleman's palace?

The writer Euripides was born in 485 B.C. and studied philosophy before writing plays. Unlike the deeply religious and more traditional playwrights Aeschylus and Sophocles, he was more of a rationalist: he believed in bringing his heroes down to earth. Not for him the grand workings of fate, rather the workings of the human mind! He wrote about 90 plays in all, of which 18 survive. The classical Greek he wrote in has a very strong meter, with lots of rhyme and assonance, but the effect of all that is lost when you translate it as prose. Recent translations have tended to be in prose, as a reaction perhaps to some of the earlier verse translations, which were in a very flowery old-fashioned style. I've done my best to avoid that and make my verse translation sound as up to date as possible, but it isn't always easy. It is of course written especially for the stage and for reading out loud.

THE ALCESTIS OF EURIPIDES

Characters of the Drama

APOLLO

DEATH

CHORUS OF THE INHABITANTS OF PHERAE

HANDMAID TO ALCESTIS

ALCESTIS

ADMETUS, KING OF PHERAE, HUSBAND OF
ALCESTIS

CHILDREN OF ADMETUS AND ALCESTIS (son and
daughter)

HERACLES

PHERES, FATHER OF ADMETUS

MOTHER OF ADMETUS (non speaking)

SERVANT

ATTENDANTS (non speaking)

The play is set in front of Admetus's palace

(Note: entrances and exits either via the palace, stage left
denoting immediate neighbourhood, or stage right
denoting from elsewhere)

Morning in front of Admetus's palace, Pherae.

Dressed in a leotard and carrying a bow and quiver full of arrows the god Apollo enters from stage left.

APOLLO   Here I am, the god Apollo,
                    Serving in Admetus' household:
                    Zeus the cause, who slew my son,
                    Asclepius, with lightning flash.
                    In revenge I killed the Cyclops,
                    Sons of Zeus who make the thunder.
                    So the father made me slave here
                    For a mortal: that's my sentence.
                    Down on earth I'm just a herdsman,
                    But my master's house I'm guarding.
                    For my master is god-fearing,
                    As befits my noble godhead.
                    So from early death I've saved him,
                    Having tricked the three fate spinners:
                    For those goddesses permitted
                    Substitution of another
                    To relieve his fated ending,
                    But appease the gods below us.
                    All his near and dear he sounded,
                    And of course his aged parents.
                    None he found who'd die in his place,
                    Giving up the sun and daylight,
                    Saving for his own dear sweet wife.
                    Now inside the house she's cradled,
                    In her time of slowly dying.
                    For this day her end is fated,
                    And this day this life's departing.

                    To escape contamination
                    I must leave this home and shelter.

Enter Death from stage right, clad in dark clothing.

                    Here comes Death. When he's approached her,
                    To the realm of Hades takes her
                    As a sacrificial victim.

65

	This the day and this the hour,
	Now appointed for her dying.
DEATH	Phoebus, Phoebus, kindly answer.
	In this house why are you lurking,
	Creeping hither, creeping thither?
	Are you trying just one more time,
	Trying to curtail and limit
	What the nether god's demanding?
	Surely it was quite sufficient
	To deflect his fatal moment,
	When you tricked those three goddesses!
	Must you stay here with your arrows
	Guarding over poor Alcestis?
	She has made her fateful promise
	That she'd die for her own husband
	To release him from his foredoom.
APOLLO	On my side are right and reason:
	You've no need to fear my motives.
DEATH	When you bring your bow and arrows,
	Can I trust your bona fides?
APOLLO	That is just my usual style.
DEATH	But I know it's your intention
	To assist this house quite wrongly.
APOLLO	When a man's my own dear good friend,
	Then of course his problems move me.
DEATH	Of a second corpse you'll rob me?
APOLLO	Did I take the first by main force?
DEATH	So how is it that he's living
	Up above ground, not below it?
APOLLO	For his wife is substituted.
	She's the one you've now come after.
DEATH	And below I'll surely take her.

APOLLO	Well then take her, as you're bidden,
	For I know I can't dissuade you.
DEATH	Not from killing who's now destined.
	It's for that we're now appointed.
APOLLO	But I'd like to try to urge you
	To kill only those who're ready.
DEATH	Now I know your rhyme and reason.
APOLLO	Please then tell me if there's someway
	She could live to see her old age.
DEATH	In my dues I gain much pleasure.
	There is no way I'd forego them.
APOLLO	But each life you take once only.
DEATH	When they're young, the honour's greater.
APOLLO	Old men's graves are so much richer.
DEATH	So it is the rich you'd favour.
APOLLO	Don't speak riddles. What's your meaning?
DEATH	Should wealth buy the right to old age?
APOLLO	Do it for me as a favour.
DEATH	No I won't, you know my methods.
APOLLO	Mortals hate them. Gods despise them.
DEATH	You can't have what is forbidden.
APOLLO	Even though you're downright savage,
	You'll be forced to stay proceedings,
	When a man comes to this household,
	Sent from wintry Thracian regions
	For a team of four fine horses.

When he's been well fed and watered,
He will seize Alcestis from you.
So in fact you'll do my bidding,
But my thanks you'll not be earning,
Hatred rather mixed with loathing.

DEATH Your words spoken much and often
Will not earn you further favours.
Down below Alcestis journeys.
With my sword I shall approach her
To begin the sacrifices.
When I've cut off someone's forelock,
To the gods below they're sacred.

Apollo and Death exit the same side they entered.
Enter the Chorus of the inhabitants of Pherae. The
chorus leader should be male.

CHORUS Before the house what means this stillness?

Why's the house in silence shrouded?

No one's here, none of his kinsmen,
Who should tell us good or bad news.
Should we mourn the poor dead princess,
Or if whether queen Alcestis,
Pelias' daughter, is still living?
Does she still behold the daylight?
All of us have one opinion
That of women she's the finest
To be born for any husband.

If events were now all over,
We'd hear sighs and lamentations,
Thudding hands within the chambers.
I don't hear them, I don't hear them.

At the outside of the palace
There aren't any servants stationed.
Mid the waves of desolation
How I pray for heaven sent healing.

Were she dead, they'd not keep silence.

But I think she's dead already.

From the house there's no announcement.

I'm afraid that doesn't prove it.

Would Admetus leave the tombstone
Of his fine and lovely mistress
Desolate of any honours?

Water for the ritual hand wash,
Executed after viewing,
Is that there beside the gate posts?

No cut locks attached to lintels
From the corpse that's plucked for mourning,
And the women's' hands aren't beating.

But today's the day appointed.

What is that you're trying to tell me?

For her journey down to Hades.

When you said that how you touched us
In our souls and deepest feelings!

When the life of good folk's taken,
Any person counted honest
Has to mourn for them sincerely.

There's no voyage which will take us
Where we might her sad life rescue.
Not the oracle in Lycia,
Nor the desert shrine of Ammon.
Her last minute now approaches.
Nothing can I give the high priest
He might offer on an altar.

Asclepius, Asclepius,
Son of Phoebus, Son of Phoebus,
Only if you were here with us,

And still saw the light of daylight,
She would leave its gloomy dwellings,
She would leave the gates of Hades.
But what hope's left for Alcestis?

For the princes all is finished
With the blood of sacrifices
On the very many altars
Sacred to the gods above us.
From our troubles there's no respite.

*A female servant comes out of the palace
weeping*

From the house a servant's coming,
And her eyes with tears are weeping.
What's the fate that I'll be hearing?
With your grief we're sympathising
For the fate of your good masters,
But there's still a hope we cherish
She's alive and has not perished.
Let us know the good or bad news.

HANDMAID   She's both dead and yet still living.

CHORUS   Can she breathe, if she's expired?

HANDMAID   Passing over, face bowed forward.

CHORUS   No hope then to stop her dying?

HANDMAID   Not when it's the fated hour,
Which compels the final moment.

CHORUS   What about the preparations?

HANDMAID   Rich tomb gifts are laid out ready
To go with her when she's buried.

CHORUS   Underneath the sun above us,
Of all women she's the finest.
She should know she dies respected.

HANDMAID She's the best, yes absolutely.
How could anyone deny it?
How could anyone surpass her?
How she honours her own husband,
When she says that she'll die for him.
Everybody round here knows it.
Marvel hearing all the actions
She inside the house accomplished:
Washed her skin in freshest water;
From the cedar wooded wardrobe
Took the dress and matching jewellery;
Dressed herself in proper fashion;
Stood in front of the hearth goddess:
Mistress, mistress how I beg you,
Down below the earth I'm going,
Kindly guard my orphaned children.
May my boy a good wife marry,
And my girl a noble husband.
May they not die prematurely,
Like their mother, but be lucky,
So they'll live a life that's pleasant
In the land of their ancestors.

Then she prayed at all the altars,
Decking them with myrtle branches.
Without tears or lamentations,
Her skin kept its fair appearance.
Next inside the bridal chamber
Fell upon the bed now weeping.
"Here, when I was still a maiden,
This was where Admetus took me,
He for whom I am now dying.
Bless this bed, should I begrudge it
That this marriage has undone me?
It is only me to perish.
Die, but don't let down my husband.
Should some other woman have you,
She could not be such a good wife,
But she might have better fortune."
Falling on the bed, she kissed it;
Sobbing on the bed, she soaked it
With the flooding of her teardrops.
Then when she could cry no longer,

71

Sprung up from it, walked bent forward,
Tried to leave the bedroom chamber,
But turned back quite time and often,
Flung herself again upon it.

Tugging at their mother's garments,
Her sweet children, weeping also,
Took them in her arms and kissed them,
First the one and then the other,
In the passion of her dying.
In the house then all the servants,
All were weeping in their pity
That they felt for their sweet mistress.
To each one she held her right hand.
No one there for being lowly
That she did not bid them farewell
And receive their fond addresses.

Those then were the awful troubles
To befall Admetus household.
Had he died, it would be over:
In escaping death's acquired
Sorrows far beyond the telling,
Far too great to be forgotten.

CHORUS   How Admetus must be groaning,
             Losing such a noble partner
             In such truly sad misfortunes.

HANDMAID In his arms he holds her to him,
             His beloved wife, Alcestis.
             How he's weeping, how he's weeping,
             Praying that he might still keep her,
             Seeking what cannot be sorted;
             For she wastes away and withers
             In a final, fatal illness.
             Yet still breathing, though quite softly,
             Though her hands just hang quite lifeless,
             Still she wants to see the sunlight,
             Though it's for the very last time.

             Specifically addressing the Chorus Leader.

I will go announce your presence.
For not all are quite so loyal
To the king and royal household
To stand kindly in these troubles,
But I know that you're an old friend
To Admetus and his family.

She goes back inside the palace.

CHORUS   Father Zeus, we do beseech you,
Who will remedy our troubles,
Who will come to save the palace,
Save it from its fate so tragic?

Who will come? Alas there's no one.
Better cut my hair in mourning,
Cloak myself in dark black raiment.

Though, dear friends, her death is certain,
To the gods we should make prayers still,
For their power is the greatest.

Asclepius, Asclepius,
For Admetus find some way out
From his sad and bitter troubles.
Please provide it, please provide it.
Once before you truly found it.
Now release her from death's journey.
Stop and check the murderous Hades.

Lost your wife then, son of Pheres,
No way can you thrive and prosper.

It's enough to cut your throat for,
Or to hang yourself from gibbet,
On this day to see his dearest,
Best beloved wife expiring.
But look, look I see her coming
From the house with her own husband.
Shout and groan, O land of Pherae,
That the finest of all women
Undergoes a wasting illness
To the nether world of Hades.

In the past I first concluded
Marriage brings more pain than pleasure.
That's the truth I can't deny it.
See our poor king's sad misfortune,
Wretched life that he'll be leading,
Now he's lost his wife the finest.

*Alcestis comes out of the palace supported by Admetus,
followed by their two children, servants and attendants*

ALCESTIS   Sun which brings us daily light,
                    Clouds which streak across the heaven.

ADMETUS   See how much we both have suffered,
                    Though the gods we ne'er offended,
                    Not to merit your now dying.

ALCESTIS   Earth and chambers of the palace,
                    Bridal suite, ancestral Iolcus.

ADMETUS   Don't give up my sad beloved,
                    Raise yourself, we then must pray for
                    Pity from the gods almighty.

ALCESTIS   On the lake a boat and oarsman
                    Comes to ferry the departed.
                    Hands on handles Charon calls me,
                    Pressing on me so impatient.
                    Hurry up, why do you linger?
                    There's no way that you can stop me.

ADMETUS   How I wish you hadn't mentioned
                    That most sad and painful journey,
                    Wretched and unlucky partner,
                    In our sufferings so bitter.

ALCESTIS   Someone leads me, someone leads me-
                    You don't see them, you don't see them-
                    To the mansions down below us,
                    Staring from his jet black eyebrows,
                    Wings outstretched, the god called Hades,
                    Let me go, let me go.

74

                    Will you stop it, please release me
                    From this wretched road I travel.

ADMETUS   Road that's truly bringing sorrow
                    To your loved ones, to your loved ones,
                    Your poor husband and poor children,
                    In the grief that we're all sharing.

ALCESTIS   Please release me, let me go now.
                    Lay me down, my strength is failing,
                    For I am so close to Hades.

                    Attendants lay her on a litter

                    Dark night creeps upon my eyelids.
                    Farewell children, farewell children,
                    You no longer have a mother,
                    But take heart, you'll still see sunlight.

ADMETUS   But your farewell is so painful,
                    Worse than many others dying.
                    Do not leave me, do not leave me.
                    By your children, who'll be orphaned,
                    Find the strength to go on living.
                    Should you die, I can't continue.
                    Live or not we are in your hands.
                    It's your love I truly worship.

ALCESTIS   Admetus, since you see the state I'm in,
                    I want to speak my mind before I die.
                    I die, because I so respected you,
                    I gave my life for you so you might live.
                    I didn't need to die on your behalf.
                    I could have had had my pick of local men,
                    To dwell in wealthy house in rich estate;
                    But couldn't bear to live if you were gone,
                    With children who were then made fatherless;
                    So didn't shrink from laying down my youth,
                    Despite the many other pleasures to be had.

                    The one who did begat you he refused,
                    Likewise the one it was who gave you birth.
                    They'd reached a time of life quite fit to die

                    75

A glorious death, if it would save their son.
For after all you were their only child.
If you were gone, what hope then would they have
To have some other children in your stead?
Our years together you and I'd see out.
You'd not lament the parting from your wife,
Nor have to raise the children on your own.
Some god has destined this, so let it be.
But don't forget the thanks you owe to us.
I do not seek an equal recompense,
For nothing is more precious than a life.
I only want what's right, you will agree.
You love the children just as much as me.
So let them stay the masters of my house,
And do not foist on them a second wife,
Who with her spite makes up for lack of class,
And lays her vicious hands upon our babes.
I beg you, please, don't even think of this.
The second wife would hate the first wife's brood
And be no kinder than a poisonous snake.
His dad will always be our dear boy's rock,
But you, my girl, how will you grow up well,
Your only hope the wife your father finds?
Back biting you when in the bloom of youth,
I hope she won't destroy your marriage chance.
No mother will attend your wedding day
Or hold your hand, when in the pains of birth.
I have to die and that means here and now:
This evil comes not in a day or two,
When I'll be spoken of among the dead.
Although we say goodbye, you must take heart.
For you my husband let it be your boast
That you were wedded to the best of wives,
And you my children's mother was the best.

CHORUS   Don't you worry, he will do this.
I don't shrink to speak up for him
All the time he's in his right mind.

ADMETUS   Yes I promise, don't you fret now,
Live or dead, my one and only
You will always be accounted:
Never will Thessalian woman
Ever call me her own husband.
None at all could ever match you,
Not in breeding or in beauty.
I have quite sufficient children.
May the gods let me enjoy **them**,
Though I'll deeply miss **your** presence.
Not for one year will my grief last,
But for my entire lifetime,
Whilst reproaching her who bore me,
And detesting my own father,
Who although they claimed to love me,
Wouldn't show it by their actions.
You, however, truly saved me,
Giving up your best possession
As a ransom for my own life.
Should I not lament my dear wife,
Losing one so truly matchless.
I shall give up holding parties,
Revels, feasting, heads in garlands.
There will be an end to music,
Though it used to fill the household.
I shall never touch the lyre,
Or uplift my mind and spirit,
Singing songs when flutes are playing;
For my life will be quite joyless,
When its source of joy's been taken.

There will be an image fashioned
Of your body, made by craftsmen
With the skills of cunning fingers.
On a bed it shall be laid out.
I shall kneel down before it.
When I clasp my arms around it,
When I call the name Alcestis,
In my mind it's you I'm holding,
My beloved, though it won't be.
It's cold comfort, well I know it,
But will ease my heartfelt sorrows.
In my dreams you'll come to see me,

And you'll cheer me well and truly.
For we know it is so pleasant
To behold a night time vision
Of the ones we love so deeply
For those moments time permits us.

Could I sing and play like Orpheus,
Then I'd charm Demeter's daughter,
Or her husband, with my music,
To recover you from Hades.
I'd go down there: who would stop me?
Not the dog that's owned by Pluto,
Nor old Charon, oars he's holding,
When he guides our souls down under,
Not before I'd brought you upward,
Back into the world of daylight.

As I can't, you must await me,
When I die, to join you thither,
And prepare for us a chamber,
Where we then can dwell together.

In these very cedar coffers
I will bid them place my body,
And to lay our bones together.
When I die, I'll not be parted,
Not from you, my one and only,
Who to me was wholly faithful.

CHORUS   As befitting any true friend,
I shall share your grief so bitter,
For she was so very worthy.

ALCESTIS   Children, children, did you hear it,
Hear your father make his promise,
So as not to disrespect me,
Not to take another woman,
To be wife and your stepmother?

ADMETUS   And again I truly say it.
It's my word, and I will keep it.

ALCESTIS   From my hands then take the children,
           If you keep to these conditions.

ADMETUS   Yes, from loving hands I take them.
           Yes, because in love they're gifted.

ALCESTIS   In my place you'll be their mother.

ADMETUS   By the force of circumstances,
           Which have robbed us of your presence.

ALCESTIS   Children, though you really need me,
           I must leave and go down under.

ADMETUS   Widowed, what on earth will I do?

ALCESTIS   Passing time will ease the burden.
           For the dead become as nothing.

ADMETUS   By the gods, please take me with you.

ALCESTIS   Just one death is quite sufficient.

ADMETUS   Oh how awful is my fortune,
           Losing such a precious partner.

ALCESTIS   When my eyes weighed down with darkness.

ADMETUS   If you leave me, I'll be ruined.

ALCESTIS   Don't address me as one living.

ADMETUS   Lift your face; don't leave your children.

ALCESTIS   Children, I don't want to leave you,
           But farewell I must now bid you.

ADMETUS   See them, see them.

ALCESTIS   I'm no longer.

ADMETUS   Are you really, really leaving?

ALCESTIS   Farewell.

ADMETUS   Wretched me, I'm undone.

CHORUS   Now she's gone and now you're widowed.

CHILD   Oh my sad fate,
Mother's passed on,
In the sunlight,
She's no longer.
Leaves me orphaned,
Leaves me wretched,
See her eyelids,
Death has closed them.
See her hands,
In rest they're laid out.
Hear and answer,
Mother, mother,
Please, I beg you,
Calling on you,
Your sweet baby.
On your lips
I fall and kiss them.

ADMETUS   But she neither sees or hears you,
In that all of us are caught up
In this tragedy so grievous.

CHILD   I am far too young, my father,
Left to go without my mother,
And be suffering these cruel mishaps.
You too have endured them with me,
You my sister. You my father,
Fruitless, fruitless was your marriage,
When you don't grow old together,
For she's perished long before you.
And, my mother, now you've passed on,
Our whole house is lost completely.

CHORUS   You must bear this fate, Admetus.
You are not the first to suffer,
Or the last of all us mortals,
Losing such a good and true wife.

ADMETUS   Truly, truly how I know it.
           This disaster was expected.
           All along indeed I saw it.
           All along how much it vexed me.

           Will you all please kindly stay here
           For the funeral arrangements.
           To the god without libation
           Down below resound your dirges.

           All Thessalians I rule over,
           Tell them share in this my mourning
           For my wife with close cropped hair cut
           And in formal dark black clothing.

           Horses which you yoke to coaches,
           Riding horses bands on foreheads
           Cut their manes with sharpest scissors.
           Ban the sound of flute or lyre
           For a twelve month in the city.

           I will never ever bury
           One whose body could be dearer,
           One whose love to me was greater,
           One more worth respect and honour,
           Since alone she died in my place.

           Alcestis is taken into the palace on the litter,
           followed by Admetus, children and attendants.

CHORUS   Daughter of Pelias,
           Down there in Hades,
           Joy we still wish you
           In sunless regions.

           They should know,
           And know it surely,
           Black haired Hades,
           Lord of Dead men,
           And that old one,
           He who's sitting
           At the helm,
           With oar and rudder,

On that rowing boat
So dreaded,
That by far
The best of women
Has now crossed
The lake of sorrow.

You'll be sung of
Time and often
To the strings
Of mountain lyres,
Or without
The help of music,
By so many
Bards and minstrels
In the cycle
Of the seasons,
When the harvest month's
Returning,
Moon that rises
For the whole night
Both on Sparta and on Athens,
Athens with its wealth so gleaming,
How, by dying,
What a theme song
You have left
For future poets.

Rowing through the Stygian waters,
Were I able, I'd return you
From the gloomy halls of Hades,
From the nether region's rivers
Back into the world of daylight.

For of women you're the dearest,
When you are the very only
Venturing to offer your life,
Rescuing your spouse from Hades.

Lightly may the earth rest on you.
If your husband takes a new bride,
Then I'd well and truly loathe him,
Just as much as would your children.

When his mother was unwilling
To go down into her coffin
As a ransom for her child,
Neither would his aged father-
He who was their very issue
They'd not save despite their grey hairs,
Resolute in lack of feeling-
You, despite your years so tender,
Passed on, dying for your husband.
Such devotion would I chance on
In my wife what a rare portion.
Truly in our life together
She would cause no painful moments.

Enter Heracles from stage right.

HERACLES   Dwellers in the land of Pherae,
Is Admetus in the palace?

CHORUS   Heracles, you'll truly find him,
In the palace that you've mentioned.
Tell us why you have come hither,
To the land of the Thessalians,
To the city walls of Pherae.

HERACLES   I'm performing one more labour,
This time for the King of Tiryns.

CHORUS   Where exactly are you going?
Are you joined in some diversion?

HERACLES   I've to take the team of horses
Which belong to Diomedes.

CHORUS   How on earth then will you do that?
Have you heard about his nature?

HERACLES   What he's like I have no inkling.
To his land I've never travelled.

CHORUS   None could ever yoke those horses,
Not without a mighty contest.

HERACLES   I could not turn down such labours.

CHORUS   It will only lead to bloodshed.
           Fresh from murder you will come back.
           Or you'll die and then remain there.

HERACLES   This is not my first such contest.

CHORUS   So, defeating Diomedes,
           What's your gain from such a battle?

HERACLES   I will then take back the horses
           To the king of the Tirynthians.

CHORUS   In their mouth to place the bridle
           You would hardly find it easy.

HERACLES   Only if they breathe out fire.

CHORUS   With their jaws so swift and savage
           They can tear a man to pieces.

HERACLES   Only mountain beasts eat people.
           Men are not the food of horses.

CHORUS   You should see their blood soaked mangers.

HERACLES   Of these fearsome steeds the keeper-
           Who's his father, so he's claiming.

CHORUS   Ares, king of golden shield.

HERACLES   This the labour that you speak of,
           It is one to which I'm fated.
           Toil and hardship I'm allotted.
           If I'm bound to join in battle
           With the children of the war god,
           With Lycaon first, then Cycnus,
           Then my third contest is surely
           Mastery of savage horses.
           None at all will ever see me
           Too afraid to join in battle,
           When my mother is Alcmene.

Admetus enters from the palace, wearing black mourning robes

CHORUS   From the palace comes Admetus,
            Lord and ruler of this country.

ADMETUS   Son of Zeus by line of Perseus,
            To my land I bid you welcome.

HERACLES   Hail to you, good king Admetus.
            Do I find you well and cheerful?

ADMETUS   Thank you kindly. Would I were so.

HERACLES   When your hair is cut in mourning.

ADMETUS   For today a corpse we bury.

HERACLES   May God grant it's not your child.

ADMETUS   In the house are both my children.

HERACLES   So perchance your aged father
            Is the one who's sadly passed on?

ADMETUS   He's alive and so's my mother.

HERACLES   Is it then your wife Alcestis?

ADMETUS   Yes and no to that's the answer.

HERACLES   Tell me if she's dead or living.

ADMETUS   She's still here and yet she isn't.
            Truly, truly how it grieves me.

HERACLES   I'm afraid I'm none the wiser,
            As it seems you're talking riddles.

ADMETUS   Do you know to what she's destined?

HERACLES   I have heard her undertaking
            That she'd die for you in your place.

ADMETUS   Well then, really, she has passed on
             From the time she made this promise.

HERACLES   Do not grieve for her beforehand.
             Put it off until the outcome.

ADMETUS   When the outcome is so certain,
             It's as if it's really happened,
             And she's dead and is no longer.

HERACLES   Not when life and death are different.

ADMETUS   Let us just agree to differ.

HERACLES   So it's someone else you're mourning.
             Was it one of your close family?

ADMETUS   It's a woman that we're mourning,
             For her death was one quite recent.

HERACLES   Close relation or a stranger?

ADMETUS   She was none of my relations,
             But connected to the household.

HERACLES   Then how was it to your household
             That she came to spend her lifetime?

ADMETUS   Orphaned, by her father dying.

HERACLES   How I wish, my dear Admetus,
             That I had not found you grieving.

ADMETUS   To what purpose your rejoinder?

HERACLES   Somewhere else I should be staying.

ADMETUS   Good sir, may the Gods forbid it.

HERACLES   When you're in a state of mourning,
             Entertaining is a burden.

86

ADMETUS	People die, so do not mind it.
	Come on in. I bid you welcome.
HERACLES	When your friend's convulsed in weeping,
	It's quite shameful to be feasting.
ADMETUS	We will take you to guest chambers
	At a distance from our quarters.
HERACLES	Let me go. I'll be most thankful.
ADMETUS	You've no need to go off elsewhere.
To a slave	You there open up the back rooms.
	Take our guest into his chambers.
	Bid the servants wine and dine him.
To others	Please close off the women's quarters.
	Feasting guests should hear no wailing,
	Nor be made to join in mourning.

Heracles exits into the palace with attendants

CHORUS	When you're in such sad misfortune
	What's the point in entertaining?
	Must you be so truly silly?
ADMETUS	What if I had then expelled him,
	Turned him from my home and kingdom,
	He who needed board and lodging,
	Would that earn your approbation?
	No it wouldn't: that's my answer.
	Would it make my troubles better
	By insulting those who visit,
	When to all our current sorrows
	We would add this further evil:
	Known abroad for lack of kindness
	To the passing guest or stranger,
	And to one who treats me grandly
	When I go to thirsty Argos?
CHORUS	But to hide your circumstances,
	If he's really such a good friend?

ADMETUS   Had he known my heart was broken,
            He would not have crossed the threshold.
            He would think my mind unbalanced,
            And I know he wouldn't praise me.
            But my house lacks all tradition
            In the sending off of strangers
            Or dishonouring our callers.

            Admetus and attendants exit inside the palace

CHORUS   In this household that's so liberal
            Lord Apollo came to live here;
            He who slew the mighty Python,
            He who plays the lyre sweetly,
            Deigned to live within its lintels,
            Deigned employment as a herdsman;
            Charmed your flocks with dulcet music,
            Songs of shepherds' love and romance.

            Just so joyous is his music
            That the spotted lynxes join them,
            Lying down with sheep and goat herd.
            Also tawny prides of lions,
            Leaving glades on Mountain Othrys,
            Dance around your lyre, Phoebus;
            Dappled fawns with graceful ankles,
            Leaping over pine tree thickets,
            In the pleasant times rejoicing.

            So the house in which you're dwelling,
            By the rippling Lake of Boebe,
            Is so wealthy in its sheep flocks,
            With ploughed fields on rich lowlands.
            Where the sun god's fearless horses
            Race off to their nighttime stables,
            That point's border: land of fresh air
            Lived in by the Molossians.
            In the east: the sea Aegean,
            Where the slopes of Mountain Pelion
            Drop so steeply there's no harbour.

            Now he opens up his household
            To receive a guest, though weeping

With wet eyes for his beloved
Wife, who is so newly passed on.
This all springs from his good breeding,
Obligation of good manners.
Those whose birth is truly noble
Act with duty that I marvel.
May my heart be ever certain
That the man who is god fearing
He will always do and fare well.

*Admetus enters from the palace, followed by the funeral
procession. Alcestis body is borne shoulder high, draped in
white robes, with jewellery and gold ornaments. Attendants
should wear black.*

ADMETUS   Kind companions gathered closely,
                Now the corpse has had due honours,
                And pall-bearers hold it upwards
                To the funeral feast and pyre,
                Will you please address the dead one,
                In accordance with our customs,
                As she goes on her last journey.

Admetus's parents enter from stage left with attendants

CHORUS   Look, here comes your aged father,
              Walking slowly with attendants,
              Bearing gifts of fine apparel
              For adornment of the funeral.

PHERES   Sympathising in your sorrows,
              Here I've come my only child.
              You have lost a wife both noble,
              Kind, composed and full of wisdom.
              But you'll have to bear this sadness,
              Though to bear it's such a burden.
              Take these gifts and let them go
              With Alcestis in her coffin.
              We must all her body worship.
              For, my son, she died in your stead,
              And she didn't leave me childless,
              In a mournful old age wasting,
              Sadly missing my dead offspring.

In her life so full of glory,
Such a model to all women,
Dared to do a deed so noble.

Farewell, for you saved my child,
Raising us when we were falling.
Even in the land of Hades
May your soul survive and prosper.
What a benefit to mortals
Does accrue from such a marriage.
Else to marry would be worthless.

ADMETUS   To this wake I didn't bid you.
In my loved ones you're not counted.
She will never wear your offering.
She needs nothing for her coffin,
Not from you or your possessions.
When you should have shown your grieving,
It was then when I was dying.
How you dare to mourn Alcestis,
When it's you who let her perish,
Though she's young, when you're so ancient.
You could not have been my father.
She could not have been my mother,
Though she's called so, claims she bore me.
But I'm sprung from lowly slave blood,
At your wife's breast substituted,
All in secret for some reason.
To the time of testing led out,
What you are you've shown quite truly.
I conclude I'm not your child.
You're the chief of spineless cowards,
When you are quite geriatric,
And your candle's nearly snuffed it,
That you wouldn't, couldn't venture
Dying for your only child,
But allowed my wife to do it,
Though she wasn't fellow kinsman.
Yet of her I think with reason
As my mother and my father.
It was such a bargain offer,
Dying for your only child,
When your life span's all but finished.

90

And I'd live my life together
With my wife, my dear Alcestis,
Not at my misfortunes moaning,
Lonesome and bereaved and parted.

When you are a man of fortune,
All the good things which are proper
You'd enjoyed them, in your kingdom
Ruling in your prime of manhood,
With a son who would succeed you,
So you wouldn't die intestate,
Leaving all your goods and chattels
To be plundered by some strangers.
Could you say you gave me over,
I who always was respectful,
To my death for bad behaviour,
In dishonouring your old age?
Quite another course of action:
My reward for filial duty
Both to you and she who bore me
Was refusal of the deal.
You must quickly have more children,
Needing health care in your dotage,
Needing them to shroud your body,
Lay your corpse out in its coffin.
My own hands just will not do this.
I'll have gone along before you.
If I chance upon a saviour,
So I'll still behold the daylight,
Of that person I'll be saying,
I'm their son and care assistant.
When you hear old people moaning,
How I wish I had passed over,
How old age is such a burden,
How their life's gone on for too long,
It's a fact they do not mean it.
When grim death is on their doorstep,
No, they want to go on living;
Though they're old, it's not a problem.

CHORUS   Stop it, you've enough misfortune.
          Must you now upset your father?

PHERES   Do you think that I'm some Phrygian
Slave you've purchased in the market
That you vex me with your nonsense?
Don't you know that I'm Thessalian,
Freeborn, truly, in my bloodstock?
Son, you really do insult me,
When you hurl at me these insults,
But by Zeus I'll have my answer.
I begat you and I raised you
To be master of this household.
But to die for you in your stead,
Tell me, where's the obligation?
Fathers dying for their children:
That's not our ancestral custom,
It's not any Greek tradition.
Long or short life, that's your own luck.
You've been handed all I owed you.
You're a king with many subjects.
All the acres of rich ploughland
Which were passed me by my father
I will leave you, unencumbered.
How on earth then have I wronged you?
Is there something I have stolen?
You'd not die in place of father:
Should I die to save my offspring?
You rejoice to see the daylight.
Should you then presume your father
Gets no pleasure from the sunrise?
Death goes on a very long time,
Spent down in the nether regions.
Life up here, though short, is sweetest.
Your attempts to put off dying:
There's no doubt they were quite shameless.
Early death for you was fated.
You contrived to go on living
By the murder of Alcestis.
Then you dare to call me coward,
You of all men quite the basest,
Put to shame by your good woman,
Dying for her fine young husband,
Who's so cleverly discovered
How to always put off dying,

When your latest wife's persuaded
To go under in your favour.
Then you rail against your family,
Just because they wouldn't do it,
When it's you that has no honour.
So I bid you, please be silent.
Think of this: you love your own life,
Don't we all, and that's the honest.
When you want to be vindictive,
You must hear the counter charges:
Though offensive, they're quite truthful.

CHORUS   Need you carry on this slander
By exchanging further libels?
Old man will you kindly stop it,
Stop insulting your own offspring!

ADMETUS   You can speak, for I have spoken,
But because the whole truth pains you,
Is no grounds to sin against me.

PHERES   If I'd died for you as bidden,
It would be a sin much greater.

ADMETUS   So you think death's just the same thing,
Whether you're a young or old man.

PHERES   One life only we're allotted:
We should not expect a second.

ADMETUS   So you'd live as long as Zeus then?

PHERES   So you'd curse your own true father,
Even though he hasn't wronged you?

ADMETUS   Yes, because you're so damn greedy,
When you want excessive long life.

PHERES   Though it's you who bears the coffin:
You're the one who should be in it.

ADMETUS   It's the proof of all your vices,
Shameless and hard-hearted coward.

PHERES   You don't have the right to say this.
            Did she perish at my instance?

ADMETUS   When you wouldn't come to help me.

PHERES   Well you better woo more women
            To die early in your favour.

ADMETUS   This serves only to reproach you,
            When you weren't prepared to do it.

PHERES   Dear to me the sun god's splendour.

ADMETUS   Inhumane your evil nature.

PHERES   When you carry my dead body,
            Maybe then you'll cease to mock me.

ADMETUS   You'll die lacking reputation,
            If of course you ever do die.

PHERES   Do you think that I'll be bothered
            Hearing slander in my coffin?

ADMETUS   Truly how it does upset me,
            When old people are so shameless.

PHERES   Poor Alcestis was not shameless,
            But alas she was quite stupid,
            So therefore you took advantage.

ADMETUS   Be off will you; let me bury her.

PHERES   I'll be off, so you can do that,
            You can bury her, you who killed her.
            You must also pay blood money,
            Compensation to her kinsmen.
            And Acastus will be no man,
            If he won't avenge his sister.

Pheres and Admetus's mother exit stage left

ADMETUS Clear off will you, with your partner.
     Live your life out, as if childless,
     Your deserts, although I'm still here.
     You'll not live with me in my house.
     If it needed proclamation
     To disown your fathers' hearthstone,
     I'd proclaim it using heralds.
     As for us, we're now departing,
     Straightway to the funeral pyre.
     For we can delay no longer
     This sad task that needs must be done.

     The funeral procession exits stage right.

CHORUS You that were so full of courage,
     Truly noble in your greatness,
     With our tears we say our farewells.
     Hermes guide you on your journey,
     With all graciousness and kindness.
     And may Hades so receive you,
     Where if good awaits the righteous,
     May you take your rightful portion,
     Sitting by his queen and consort.

     A s*ervant enters from the palace.*

SERVANT Many guests from every country
     Have been welcomed in this palace:
     I have served them all their dinner.
     Never yet a guest that's ruder
     Have I waited on than this one.
     Though he sees my master's mourning,
     Firstly comes inside the palace,
     Then he quite forgets his manners-
     Never mind the circumstances-
     With regard to what he's given.
     But if something's not been brought him,
     Then he orders us to fetch it.
     Fills an ivy bowl with liquor,
     From the mother grape extracted,
     Drinks and drinks it till his system's
     So suffused with fiery spirit

His whole body's over heating.
On his head are myrtle branches,
From his mouth comes raucous singing.
You can hear two different theme songs.
Whilst he howls his filthy ditties,
Quite ignoring all our sorrows,
We're lamenting our dead mistress.
But our tears are kept in secret
From our guest. Admetus told us.
In the house I'm left to wait on
This our guest, this no good waster,
Whilst her corpse has left the palace.
I can't hail her or lament her.
She was like a mother to us,
Saving us from many sorrows,
When she soothed her husband's temper.
At this time of much misfortune,
Aren't I justified in hating,
This unwanted guest who's turned up.

*Enter a drunken Heracles from the palace, wreath of flowers
on head.*

HERACLES   You there, you're so awfully solemn,
And your mind is somewhere else, sir.
When you're only just a servant,
You've no business to be sullen
To your master's guests, so cheer up,
Welcome them with warm demeanour:
I'm Admetus' bosom buddy.
Therefore you should not receive me
With black looks and furrowed frowning,
Mind set on external problems.
Come to me for words of wisdom.
Man's estate: you know its nature.
I don't think so. Why? Just hear me.
All of flesh and blood die some day.
There's no way that mortals can know
Whether they will live tomorrow.
Where on earth our fate will lead us,
No one knows and none can teach us,
Or divine by art or science.
Now you've heard and learnt this message,

It's high time for you to cheer up.
Drink and look to this day only;
Leave the rest to chance and fortune.
Sweetest of the gods is Cypris.
She's so kindly, so respect her.
You can disregard all others.
Trust me if you think I'm talking
Sense-I'm sure you really do so.
Lift all cares from off your shoulders.
Drink with us, bedecked in garlands,
Rise above all earthly problems.

Dip your oars inside the goblet.
It's a boat you'll tumble into,
Casting off from grief and sorrow,
Everything that makes you gloomy.
Mortals should be philosophic
With regard to matters mortal.
In my humble estimation
Those who frown and are so solemn
Don't enjoy their life one minute,
Which is just one long disaster.

SERVANT   No need to tell us this, we know it,
But it's not the time to tell us.
We're engaged on other matters,
Which preclude all fun and laughter.

HERACLES   But she wasn't your relation.
Do not over do the mourning,
When the rulers of this household
Lord and Lady still enjoy life.

SERVANT   How on earth can they enjoy life?
Don't you know our present sorrows?

HERACLES   Has your master then misled me?

SERVANT   To his guests he's over friendly.

HERACLES   For a stranger's death, however,
I should not forego my pleasures.

SERVANT   If she truly were a stranger.

HERACLES   So he's kept this secret from me,
           Just what tragic fate befalls him.

SERVANT   You can go your way rejoicing.
           We will mind our master's sorrows.

HERACLES   Judging by the words you're speaking,
           You're not mourning someone distant.

SERVANT   I assure you, if I were so,
           Your carousing wouldn't pain me.

HERACLES   Should I blame my bad behaviour
           On my host who quite misled me?

SERVANT   It was not the proper moment
           To be welcomed in this household,
           For we're in a state of mourning.
           You can tell from what we're wearing,
           Dark black clothes with shaven forelocks.

HERACLES   Who's passed on? Will someone tell us?
           My host's child or his father?

SERVANT   Honoured guest, his wife Alcestis.

HERACLES   Is this true? You really mean it,
           Yet you deigned to entertain me.

SERVANT   To have barred you from his household
           Was an act to him quite shameful.

HERACLES   How I pity poor Admetus,
           Losing such a perfect partner.

SERVANT   We're all lost, we're dead beside her.

HERACLES   I'm a fool, I should have realised,
           When I saw his crying eyelids,
           Downcast face and cut off forelocks,
           But he really did convince me

It was someone unconnected
They were taking to be buried.
Entering the royal palace,
Quite against my better judgement,
I got drunk inside the chambers
Of my host who made me welcome,
In despite his circumstances.
Then I really did get merry,
With my head bedecked in garlands.
And you weren't allowed to tell me,
Though surrounded in the household,
By the depths of such misfortune.
Will you tell me where she's buried,
Where to go to find her coffin.

SERVANT   You will see her marble tombstone
Close by where you leave the city,
On the straight road to Larissa.

HERACLES   Heart of mine, that's much enduring,
And my hands, you have to show now,
What a son Alcmene bore to
Zeus, when she from Tiryns hails,
And Electryon's her father.
For I have to go and rescue
Alcestis, who's newly passed on,
Bring her right back to this palace,
As a favour for Admetus.
I've to find the King of Corpses,
Black-robed Death, and where I'll find him,
By the tomb, libations drinking.
I will lie in wait in ambush.
Springing up, I then will seize him.
In a firm embrace I'll grasp him.
No one else could then release him,
Whilst his ribs are crushed so strongly,
Till to me he frees Alcestis.
If alas I miss my quarry,
Where for sacrificial offerings
Blood is mingled, but he comes not,
To the sunless halls I'm going
Of King Hades and his girl bride.
I shall beg them and persuade them

99

I should bring Alcestis upwards,
Place her in my dear host's own hands,
He who in his house received me,
Did not turn me out though broken,
By a tragedy so painful.
For respect he hid it from me,
Obligated by good manners.
Who on earth could show more kindness
To their guests than ever he did,
Who in Thessaly or Hellas?
I must then return the favour
From my sense of shame and honour.

Exits inside palace
Admetus and mourners return

ADMETUS   The palace now has lost its mistress.
I can't bear to journey to it.
I can't bear to look upon it.
In my sadness how I feel it,
At a loss for speech or action,
Where to go in my undoing.
I was born to sorrow destined.
How I envy all who've perished,
How I wish that I had joined them
In the underworld's dark hallways.
I've no pleasure from the sunrise.
I've no pleasure from earth's soil.
I've no wish to stand upon it.
For I've lost my Queen Alcestis,
Death has taken her a hostage
To the chambers dark of Hades.

CHORUS   Please Admetus, in your interests,
Hide yourself inside the palace.

ADMETUS   How bitter my sorrows.

CHORUS   That you cry out's not surprising,
When we think of what you've suffered,
Pain and sorrow that you've gone through.

ADMETUS   Oh my anguish, oh my anguish.

CHORUS   Does not help her down in Hades.

ADMETUS   Alas, alas.

CHORUS   It is truly, truly grievous,
           That you'll never see the sweet face
           Of your wife so well beloved.

ADMETUS   Now you've said it, now you've said it.
           That's what makes it so, so bitter.
           Of all evils for us mortals,
           Far the worst's to lose your partner,
           When your partner's been so faithful.
           Would to God we hadn't married,
           Lived together in this palace.
           Those unmarried with no children
           Them I envy, them I envy.
           They've but one life to watch over.
           In that life's sufficient anguish,
           Makes its grief a modest burden.
           Children sick with raging fevers,
           Death devouring wedding partners-
           Who on earth would choose to see it,
           If they could have stayed unmarried,
           Not had children, for their whole life?

CHORUS   This sad fate that's come upon us

ADMETUS   Hard it is to wrestle with it.

CHORUS   Though your grief is truly painful,
           You must place a limit on it.

ADMETUS   That I cannot.

CHORUS   Must endure it.
           Though it's harsh, you're not the first one,
           Not the first to lose a good wife.
           Many other troubles also
           Crush upon the lot of mortals.

101

ADMETUS   Oh how great the grief and mourning,
When your loved one's passed down under.
In the hollow pit that's channelled
For her coffin, what's to stop me
Diving in it, self destroying,
To lie with my wife most noble?
Hades then would have our both lives,
Two not one who were most faithful,
Two who crossed the lake together
To his subterranean kingdom.

CHORUS   There was someone in my family
Who had just an only child.
Good and noble was his one son,
But alas he died quite early
In the homestead of his father.
Now bereft of a successor,
None the less he took it calmly,
Though already quite an old man,
With his hair turned grey and silver.

ADMETUS   How to go into
My sad empty palace,
How shall I live there,
Now that my life's changed?
Such is the difference.
Bearing pine fronds from
The mountain of Pelion,
With wedding tunes
I entered in there,
Holding the hands of
My dear and true wife.
Revellers followed,
Noisy, loud sounding,
Calling us happy,
Me and my dead wife,
From noble families
Both sides descended,
So yoked together.
But now instead of
Songs, there's just mourning,
Black robes for white gowns,

Sending me inside
To lonely bedroom.

CHORUS   You enjoyed the best of fortune,
Quite unused to pain and sorrow,
When this tragic blow befell you,
But you're still alive and breathing.
Though your wife is now departed,
Yet remains her true affection.
This is not a new misfortune.
Death before has robbed so many
Of their wives so good and faithful.

ADMETUS   Friends, you really wouldn't think it
That my wife's fate is much better
Than the lot that I'm enduring,
But in fact that's my opinion.
For no pain will ever touch her,
And with glorious reputation
She has ceased from every trouble.
As for me, who should not be here,
Going past my proper portion,
I will live a life that's grievous.
Now at last I've come to see it.

Ways in the palace
How shall I bear them?
Who shall I speak to,
Or to reply to,
Giving me pleasure
In comings and goings?
Where shall I turn to?
For the loneliness inside the palace,
The sight of my wife's empty bed chamber,
The dusty dry floors throughout the hallways,
The chairs she sat on are driving me out,
As when my children weep for their mother,
Falling at my knees, and servants mourning
Their mistress lost with charge of the
household.
But worse is to come outside the palace,
Where Thessalian weddings assail me,
Gatherings of women, how can I bear it,

103

To look at those the age of my lost wife?
And when they slander me, those who hate me,
"Just look at him whose life's so disgraceful,
Couldn't bear dying and so escaped Hades,
Gave in exchange the one whom he married,
Call him a man when he's such a coward,
And puts the blame on both of his parents."
Adds to my sorrows bad reputation.
What's to gain, friends, to live my life that
way?
Bad words I'm hearing, badly I'm faring.

CHORUS   Soaring upwards,
Fate is strongest,
I've determined
From my studies,
Art and music,
Books and writing.

To Fate no antidote's discovered,
Written on those Thracian tablets,
By the hand and voice of Orpheus,
Nor from medicines Phoebus issued
To the children of Asclepius
For the many cares of mortals.

Fate alone she has no idols-
Fate alone she has no altars-
And receives no sacrifices.
Do not come to me, Queen Goddess,
Showing any stronger powers.
Whatsoever Zeus determines
With your help it comes to being:
You have force to temper steel,
And to conquer stubborn natures.
In her hands she surely took you,
In her fetters tightly bound you.
Just be brave and show your courage.
Weeping as we are above ground
For the dead who are below ground
With regret will not return them.
To the realm of death pass also
Children sired by immortals,

Secretly on mortal women.
When alive we truly loved her,
So in death we won't forget her,
Of all wives by far the finest.

Let her tomb be not regarded
As the mound on some dead body,
But a shrine for pilgrim travellers,
Who consider her a goddess.
When they veer off from the main road,
They will say when they will behold it:
Then she died to save her husband,
Now she is a saint most blessed.
Queen, farewell, in turn please bless us,
Such the prayers which will address you.

Admetus, see Alcmene's offspring,
Who now comes unto your hearthstone.

*Heracles enters from stage right leading Alcestis by the hand,
but her face is completely hidden by a veil.*

HERACLES   To a man who is my best friend
It behoves to speak quite freely.
I should not keep dumbly silent
Through deep seated inhibition.
Rather, in your present troubles,
I'd be counted true and steadfast.
In your house you entertained me,
Notwithstanding your deceased wife,
Practising polite deception
That the corpse was someone distant.
Festal garlands on my forehead,
To the gods I poured libations
Mid the sorrows of your household.
Thus deluded, I should fault find,
But don't wish to cause you anguish
In your troubles. Why I've come here,
Steps retracing, I will tell you.
Take this woman: keep her for me,
Till I'm back with Thracian horses,
Having killed the king of Biston.
If perchance a sadder outcome,

Though I'm sure return is certain,
You may keep her as a servant.
I obtained her, as a prize won,
In a public competition
Certain persons had enacted:
Tasks quite worthy of good athletes.
If you ran, the prize was horses.
In the harder martial contests,
Strength of arm to box and wrestle,
Prize awarded: yoke of oxen,
But with them a woman followed.
Since I happened just to be there,
To pass by this prize so splendid
Really would have been quite shameful.
As I said, please kindly mind her.
Be assured I have not snatched her.
In a trial of strength I won her,
And in time you'll come to praise me.

ADMETUS   Hardly wishing to insult you,
Or to make you act through error,
In a way that might disgrace you,
Did I hide my wife's sad fortune.
But it would have further grieved me,
Had you gone off to stay elsewhere.
Should you have to mind my sorrows?
But, good sir, if there's a slight chance
You can find another minder
From the ranks of all Thessalians,
Someone who's not had my problems,
I suggest you kindly ask them.
Surely many are located
Mid the dwellers here in Pherae?
Don't remind me of my troubles.
Seeing her inside the palace,
I could hardly stop from crying.
Do not add to my deep sadness.
I'm weighed down in this disaster.
I have quite sufficient problems.
Where besides should she be stationed
In the palace, this young lady?
Young she seems by what she's wearing.
Could she dwell in male quarters?

Moving there among the young men,
She could hardly stay a virgin.
Heracles, it's not so easy,
Warding off those fit young males.
I must surely mind your interests.
Or perhaps in my wife's chamber
I should enter in and keep her,
Let her lie on my wife's mattress.
I would earn twofold reproachment,
From the locals who'd accuse me
Of betraying my dear late wife,
When she'd laid her life down for me,
Taking on another partner,
And from dead Alcestis also,
She who's worthy of my worship.
This requires utmost caution.
Woman, who you are I know not,
But you are the very shape of
Dear Alcestis and the same size,
And by God you're like her also.
From my sight you must remove her.
For she'll surely take me captive.
When I see her, then it seems that
It's my wife that I am seeing.
My heart thumps and beats much faster.
From my ears salt tears are pouring,
I, who am so truly wretched,
Having tasted grief so bitter.

CHORUS I could hardly praise your fortune,
But no matter what's our station,
What the gods send, we must take it.

HERACLES If I had such mighty powers,
I could summon back your dead wife
From the regions down below us
To the world of light and sunshine,
That's the favour I would do you.

ADMETUS Yes of course you'd want to do that.
That I know both well and truly.
Where and how that is the problem,
For the dead don't come back upwards.

HERACLES   So don't overdo your grieving.
            Try to bear your troubles lightly.

ADMETUS   Yes, to give advice is easy,
            But to bear misfortune's harder.

HERACLES   What's to gain by non-stop mourning?

ADMETUS   Yes I hear you, but love makes me.

HERACLES   Makes you tearful, love for dead one.

ADMETUS   Love for dead one has destroyed me.
            Far, far more than words can utter.

HERACLES   That you've lost a noble woman-
            There is none that can deny it.

ADMETUS   So my life has no enjoyment.

HERACLES   Though your grief is young and bitter,
            In the long run time will heal it.

ADMETUS   All the time till my death also
            Is the long run time requires.

HERACLES   Love and yearning for a new bride
            Will suffice to cease your anguish.

ADMETUS   Don't say that: I'd never think it.

HERACLES   But why not? Your bed is empty,
            And you're free to be re-married.

ADMETUS   There's no woman I'd lie next to.

HERACLES   Let me ask you. How will that help
            Your dead wife, who's now departed?

ADMETUS   Where she is, I must respect her.

HERACLES Whilst I hear your views and praise them,
          Some would say you are quite foolish.

ADMETUS   And they'll never call me bridegroom.

HERACLES You're so constant I admire it.

ADMETUS   Die I'd rather than betray her.

HERACLES Now inside your house receive her.

ADMETUS   In the name of Zeus your father,
          Do not force this deed upon me.

HERACLES But I tell you, you should do it.
          You'd be wrong to so decline her.

ADMETUS   If I did it, grief would sting me.

HERACLES Trust me: joy will fall upon you.

ADMETUS   How I wish you had not won her
          In the contest you referred to.

HERACLES You were equal victor with me.

ADMETUS   You have spoken with persuasion,
          But the woman must be let go.

HERACLES Though she'll go away if needful,
          First of all see if she must go.

ADMETUS   Even though it makes you angry,
          She must go away. I mean it.

HERACLES But because I have first seen her,
          I am eager she should stay here.

ADMETUS   Well all right; but she'll not please me.

HERACLES But you'll come to praise me for this.
          So meanwhile you should trust me.

ADMETUS   In the house then, servants, take her.

HERACLES   To attendants I'll not hand her.

ADMETUS   Well then take her, you in person.

HERACLES   It's your hands that should receive her.

ADMETUS   Though she goes inside the palace,
           With my hands I shall not touch her.

HERACLES   Only your right hand should touch her.

ADMETUS   Sir, you're forcing me to do this,
           Much against my inclination.

HERACLES   Hold your hand out: touch the lady.

ADMETUS   But averting my gaze from her,
           As if fighting with a Gorgon.

HERACLES   Do you hold her?

ADMETUS   Yes, I do so.

           He holds her hand, but does not look at her.

HERACLES   Well from henceforth you must keep her,
           And extol your noble house guest.
           Please examine her quite closely,
           If she looks like your Alcestis,
           And you can your grief abandon
           With this change in fate and fortune.

ADMETUS   Gods above, what shall I utter,
           What an unexpected wonder,
           To behold again my true love,
           Or that this joy's just illusion,
           Jest of some god who must mock me?

HERACLES   No, it's not. You see your own wife.

ADMETUS   Not some phantom from the dead world?

110

HERACLES	Do I conjure up dead spirits? Is this guest a necromancer?
ADMETUS	But when she is dead and buried, In the flesh how can I see her?
HERACLES	That you see her is quite certain. That you disbelieve your fortune Does not give me cause to marvel.
ADMETUS	Do you mean that I can touch her, Talk to my wife as still living?
HERACLES	Talk to her, of course, you're welcome. You have all you ever wanted.
ADMETUS	Form and face of my beloved, Back against all expectation, When I never thought to see you, In my arms I firmly hold you.
HERACLES	Yes, you hold her, and may no god Bear you ill will for good fortune.
ADMETUS	Well born son of Zeus almighty, May you prosper in your ventures, And may Zeus both guard and keep you, You who have restored my fortunes, Bringing her back to the daylight, From the underworld below us. Tell me, just how did you do it?
HERACLES	Battling with the Lord of Spirits.
ADMETUS	With grim death engaged in contest, Where took place this fearsome conflict?
HERACLES	From an ambush by the tombstone, With my hands I firmly grasped him.
ADMETUS	But why does she stay quite silent?

HERACLES   It's not right for you to hear her,
           Not while she's still consecrated
           To the deities below us.
           Not till that's been countermanded,
           And the dawning of the third day.
           Take her back inside the palace.
           You're a just man. So continue,
           In respect of guests and strangers.
           Fare you well, I'm on my journey
           To perform allotted labour
           For Sthenelus royal offspring.

ADMETUS   Please stay on, and share our hearthstone.

HERACLES   In the future I will do that,
           But for now departure hastens.

ADMETUS   May good luck attend you always.
           May you come back to my palace.
           All the freemen of these kingdoms
           I shall bid to set up dances,
           To mark out this happy fortune,
           And to make the altars smoking,
           Sacrificing slaughtered oxen,
           To the gods in supplication.
           For our life we're re-arranging,
           Far, far better than before-times
           In affirming our good fortune.

           All except the chorus enter the palace.

CHORUS   Fate has many shapes and guises.
           Much the gods bring unexpected.
           What we planned for doesn't work out.
           By the hands of the Immortal
           Comes to pass what least we hoped for.
           That's the story we've just told you.

                         THE END

                           112